Bounty of BILTMORE COOKBOOK

A recipe collection
from Biltmore Estate
Asheville, North Carolina

Grilled Teriyaki Pork Chops with
Summer Peach Salsa, page 109

Bounty of BILTMORE COOKBOOK

Compiled and edited by
Whitney Wheeler Pickering

Oxmoor
House.

©2000 by Oxmoor House, Inc.
Book Division of Southern Progress Corporation
P.O. Box 2463, Birmingham, Alabama 35201

Library of Congress Catalog Card Number: 99-76970
ISBN: 0-8487-1955-7

Printed in the United States of America
Second Printing 2000

Editor-in-Chief: Nancy Fitzpatrick Wyatt
Senior Foods Editor: Susan Payne Stabler
Senior Editor, Copy and Homes: Olivia Kindig Wells
Art Director: James Boone

Bounty of Biltmore Cookbook
Editor: Whitney Wheeler Pickering
Copy Editor: Cathy Ritter Scholl
Editorial Assistant: Allison Long
Director, Test Kitchens: Kathleen Royal Phillips
Assistant Director, Test Kitchens: Gayle Hays Sadler
Test Kitchens Staff: Julie Christopher, Gretchen Feldtman, Natalie E. King,
         Rebecca Mohr, Jan A. Smith, Kate M. Wheeler, R.D.
Senior Photographer: Jim Bathie
Photographer: Brit Huckabay
Senior Photo Stylist: Kay E. Clarke
Publishing Systems Administrator: Rick Tucker
Director, Production and Distribution: Phillip Lee
Associate Production Manager: Theresa L. Beste
Production Assistant: Faye Porter Bonner

Contributors:
Designer: Carol Damsky
Writer: Judy Ross
Editorial Assistants: Sally Inzer, Courtney Hughes
Indexer: Mary Ann Laurens
Test Kitchens Staff: Shelley Clayton, Jon Dubay, Lorrie Hulston,
         Leigh Mullinax
Biltmore Estate Project Coordinators: Executive Chef Stephen Adams,
         Christina Cowan, Jane Cox Murray, Barbara O'Neil, Elizabeth Pendleton

Biltmore Estate is open to visitors daily except for
Thanksgiving and Christmas days.

For ticket information call
800-543-2961 • www.biltmore.com

To receive additional copies of this book,
please call 800-968-0558.

Cover: Fresh Mozzarella-Tomato-Basil Salad, *page 132*

CONTENTS

A PERSONAL REFLECTION

When my great-grandfather invited his family and friends to visit his country home, guests often spent weeks at Biltmore Estate. Fine food and wine were a major part of their experience, starting with breakfast in bed served on silver trays. The day might continue with lunch in the Morning Room, afternoon tea in the Tapestry Gallery, an elaborate black-tie dinner in the Banquet Hall, ending with a nightcap in the Library.

Back then, much of the food served to Biltmore visitors was raised on Estate farms. By my great-grandfather's design, Biltmore Estate strives for self-sufficiency, thereby ensuring guests receive the freshest foods of the season.

This legacy of self-sufficiency continues even today. While multicourse meals have now been replaced with more casual dining, we value variety, freshness, and high-quality foods more than ever. The chefs in Biltmore Estate's three signature restaurants have apprenticed in fine kitchens around the country and work in tandem with our agricultural staff and our European-trained winemakers to determine what will appear on future menus. This collaboration inspires creative cuisine which never fails to please.

I am glad to share some of their recipes and experience with you, and invite you to return often to taste the bounty of Biltmore.

William A.V. Cecil, Jr.
Chief Executive Officer
The Biltmore Company

From Biltmore Estate's beginning in the 1890's—before the gracious gardens were carefully planted, even before the 250-room French Renaissance château was completed—delicious homegrown food played an important role in Estate life.

George Washington Vanderbilt conceived Biltmore Estate on the European model of a self-sufficient country property, an ideal he had observed on his travels. Old farms existed in the Blue Ridge Mountains of Asheville, North Carolina, among the 125,000 acres Vanderbilt amassed. Although the land had been overlogged and overworked for generations, Vanderbilt and his landscape architect, Frederick Law Olmsted, thought that proper care could restore the earth to a more fruitful state.

As work progressed on Biltmore House, Olmsted advocated agricultural endeavors along the rich river bottoms. A vegetable garden and dairy were established to provide food for Estate workers and income for the expanding construction project.

George W. Vanderbilt

Once the House was completed, Vanderbilt and his guests enjoyed the Estate's bounty: fresh vegetables, fruits, grain crops, meat and dairy products, and honey from 41 beehives. Eggs, milk, butter, and cheese from Biltmore Estate were sold in Asheville and throughout the Southeast. After the Estate opened to the public, the Biltmore Dairy Bar—located next to the main dairy building—became known for its delicious ice cream specialties.

CONTINUING VANDERBILT'S LEGACY

When George and Edith Vanderbilt entertained guests, eight-course dinners in the Banquet Hall were served by uniformed footmen, requiring 15 utensils per person. Although dining at Biltmore Estate

Visitors to the Walled Garden today may find it difficult to picture it as a vegetable and fruit garden. Now sheltering thousands of spring bulbs, summer roses, and autumn chrysanthemums, the Garden was designed by Frederick Law Olmsted for growing choice fruits and vegetables in addition to flowers. George Vanderbilt overruled his expert, preferring "a garden of ornament rather than utility," and designated the surrounding farmland for crop production.

remains a cherished tradition, the meals and preparation have changed with modern tastes, utilizing fresh foods and simpler techniques.

The legacy of the land continues at Biltmore, carried on by the Vanderbilts' great-grandson, William A. V. Cecil, Jr., chief executive officer of The Biltmore Company. The family has championed efforts to expand the guest experience into fine dining using Estate-raised products and Biltmore Estate wines.

At our restaurants, guests indulge in innovative menus prepared by chefs focused on seasonality, choosing vegetables, herbs, meat, and fruit grown on the Estate and harvested at the peak of flavor. Abundance in the surrounding gardens, fields, and orchards inspires our chefs: vine-ripened tomatoes, crisp salad greens, shiitake mushrooms, plump, juicy raspberries and blackberries, Angus beef, and spring lamb find their way into their creative cuisine.

The Bistro, located at the Winery, features European-influenced appetizers, elegant entrées, gourmet pizzas baked in a wood-fired oven, and decadent desserts served in an airy and bright atmosphere. Handmade pastas topped with grilled vegetables, tasty focaccia, and Biltmore-raised beef flavor the menu at lunch and dinner.

The Stable Café, located next to Biltmore House, inhabits the renovated stables that once kept George Vanderbilt's prize horses. Simple, hearty meals, sandwiches, and salads utilize fresh local ingredients for casual lunches—topped off with delectable desserts.

Deerpark Restaurant is noted for bountiful buffets laden with Southern specialties. Delicious main dishes often feature rainbow trout, accompanied by seasonal vegetables, puddings, and fresh berry cobblers.

Estate-Raised Quality

*B*iltmore's farm program supplies the Estate's three restaurants, with some items sold at local retail stores. Agricultural efforts include:
- *Blackberries—test plots are determining which types perform best.*
- *Blueberries—nine varieties of rabbiteye and highbush are grown.*
- *Cattle—registered Angus and Limousin cattle produce beef and veal.*
- *Grain crops—corn and other grains are grown for livestock feed.*
- *Grapes—more than 48,000 vines yield 350 tons of Chardonnay, Cabernet Sauvignon, Cabernet Franc, Riesling, Pinot Noir, Merlot, and Viognier grapes in a good year.*
- *Lambs—Dorset and Dorper breeds produce lambs year-round to extend availability (and the wool is collected during the year and sold at a local wool market).*
- *Raspberries—eight varieties of red and yellow fruits are harvested June through October; additional fruit is sold in local grocery stores under the Biltmore Estate label.*
- *Garden Vegetables—more than 100 varieties of vegetables and herbs are grown in the 8.25-acre Market Garden.*

As part of the Estate's self-sufficiency, the Biltmore Estate Winery opened in 1985 to produce European-style wines. The Winery yields more than 75,000 cases of wine each year, aided by guests who help harvest 73 acres of grape vines planted on the Estate's west side. Chardonnay, Cabernet Sauvignon, Cabernet Franc, and Riesling are among the varieties growing well in the temperate mountain climate. After the harvest, in a renovated facility once housing the dairy's calving barn, Biltmore's winemaker blends science and artistry into award-winning wines marketed under the BILTMORE ESTATE®, Château Biltmore®, and GWV® (for George Washington Vanderbilt) brands.

> *Guests who dine at Biltmore Estate benefit from its heritage of hospitality, which flavors each season*

SEASONS OF SPLENDOR

Guests who dine at Biltmore Estate benefit from its heritage of hospitality, which flavors each season with a unique blend of fresh foods, historic ambience, and gracious service.

Spring brings renewed growth and vitality to the land at Biltmore Estate. Biltmore House is elaborately decorated with Gilded Age floral arrangements, and the breathtaking Gardens feature weekend music and entertainment. In keeping with this time of renewal, our chefs develop menus utilizing springtime specialties such as lamb and cool-season vegetables.

In summer, guests enjoy pleasant diversions on walking trails and in the rose-filled Walled Garden. The vegetable garden is in full production, offering

Early morning in the Biltmore Estate Vineyard

healthy choices and lighter fare. *Summer Evenings Concerts*, held on the South Terrace of Biltmore, are perfect reasons for festive picnics. At the Winery, summer holiday weekends bring jazz and tips on outdoor entertaining.

As the mountain breezes hint of cool days and nights, harvest time approaches. Fall foliage and a carpet of vivid chrysanthemums draw guests to breathtaking vistas. Biltmore's bounty is celebrated during *Michaelmas: An English Harvest Fair*, commemorating the abundance of the land with a turn-of-the-century festival featuring lively music, entertainment, and arts and crafts demonstrations.

Christmas at Biltmore Estate offers splendor reminiscent of Christmas Eve 1895, when George Vanderbilt welcomed family members to his new home. Dozens of stately trees, hundreds of fresh wreaths and poinsettias, and miles of garland adorn the Estate. *Candlelight Christmas Evenings* provide a unique view of the House's ornate decorations and exquisite artwork. Choirs and musical ensembles add to the holiday spirit. Elaborate meals featuring traditional favorites tempt guests at the Estate's restaurants.

In winter, after the frenetic pace of the holidays has eased, there's time to appreciate the artistic treasures found within Biltmore House. These quieter moments invite guests to peruse Vanderbilt's home at a more leisurely pace; cozy, hearty meals chase winter's chill.

A Year's Bounty from the Market Garden

- *Asparagus: green, purple, white*
- *Bell peppers: red, green*
- *Broccoli*
- *Broccoli raab*
- *Cabbage: bok choy, green, Napa, red*
- *Carrots: Thumbelina baby round*
- *Cauliflower*
- *Celeriac*
- *Corn*
- *Fruit trees: Fuji apple, pawpaw, Japanese persimmon*
- *Gourds: decorative including birdhouse, dipper, large kettle*
- *Herbs: calendula, chives, chocolate mint, curly parsley, dill, fennel, garlic chives, green basil, Italian parsley, lavender, oregano, peppermint, pineapple sage, purple basil, rosemary, spearmint, thyme*
- *Kale: green*
- *Lettuce: green butterhead, red butterhead, green leaf, red leaf, green oakleaf, red oakleaf, green romaine, red romaine*
- *Peas: sugarsnap*
- *Pumpkins: giant, miniature, white*
- *Scallions: red, green*
- *Shiitake mushrooms*
- *Spinach*
- *Squash: green acorn, green scallop, yellow scallop, yellow crookneck, spaghetti, zucchini, baby squash with blooms, squash blossoms*
- *Strawberries: red alpine, yellow alpine*
- *Swiss chard: red, "Brite lights," yellow lights*
- *Tomatoes: Big Beef, cherry, green, yellow pear, red, red pear, Roma*

Menus for
ALL SEASONS

EASTER CELEBRATION

Hearts of Palm Salad with
Bell Pepper Vinaigrette

Mint-Crusted Rack of Lamb

Lemon Couscous

Buttered Baby Carrots

Basil Batter Rolls

⚜ *Château Biltmore Cabernet Sauvignon*

Fresh Strawberry Napoleons

⚜ *Biltmore Estate Blanc de Blanc-Sec*

Serves 4

HEARTS OF PALM SALAD
WITH BELL PEPPER VINAIGRETTE

Hearts of palm are actually the edible inner "heart" of the stem of the cabbage palm tree. The flavor of this edible tree portion is very delicate and much like that of the artichoke. Most of the hearts of palm that are enjoyed in the U.S. are either from Florida, where the cabbage palm tree is the state tree, or from Brazil.

1 large head romaine lettuce

1 (14-ounce) can hearts of
    palm, drained and sliced
    into ½-inch rings

Bell Pepper Vinaigrette

WASH, trim, and tear enough lettuce to make 6 cups.

ARRANGE lettuce and hearts of palm on 4 serving plates, if desired. Serve with vinaigrette. **Yield:** 4 servings.

Deerpark Restaurant: Chef's Choice
BELL PEPPER VINAIGRETTE

⅓ cup olive oil

⅓ cup cider vinegar

¼ cup diced green bell pepper

¼ cup diced yellow bell pepper

¼ cup diced red bell pepper

¼ cup diced onion

¼ cup cold water

1 tablespoon sugar

1 tablespoon minced garlic

1½ teaspoons chopped fresh
    parsley

1½ teaspoons chopped fresh
    thyme

¼ teaspoon salt

¼ teaspoon black pepper

COMBINE all ingredients in a bowl, and stir with a wire whisk until well blended. **Yield:** 1⅔ cups.

MINT-CRUSTED RACK OF LAMB

2 (8-rib) lamb rib roasts (1½ pounds each), trimmed
1 teaspoon salt
½ teaspoon pepper
2 cups French bread cubes
¼ cup butter or margarine, softened
¼ cup lemon juice
¼ cup chopped fresh parsley
½ cup chopped fresh mint
2 cloves garlic, minced
¼ cup stone-ground Dijon mustard

SPRINKLE lamb with salt and pepper. Cook lamb in a large nonstick skillet over medium-high heat 3 to 4 minutes on each side or until browned.

PROCESS bread and next 5 ingredients in a food processor until coarsely ground. Brush mustard over lamb; press breadcrumb mixture over mustard. Place lamb on a lightly greased rack in a broiler pan.

BAKE at 400° for 40 to 45 minutes or until a meat thermometer inserted into thickest portion registers 145° (internal temperature will rise upon standing).

REMOVE from oven, and let stand 5 minutes or until thermometer registers 150° (medium rare.) **Yield:** 4 to 6 servings.

LEMON COUSCOUS

A tiny grain, couscous cooks quickly, absorbing flavors from the broth in which it's cooked. Here, the zing of lemon rind and freshly squeezed lemon juice enhances its flavor.

1 cup chicken broth
1 tablespoon grated lemon rind
2 tablespoons fresh lemon juice
1 tablespoon butter or margarine
¼ teaspoon salt
⅔ cup couscous, uncooked
2 tablespoons pecan pieces, toasted
2 tablespoons chopped fresh parsley

COMBINE first 5 ingredients in a saucepan; bring to a boil. Add couscous, stirring well; cover, remove from heat, and let stand 5 minutes. Fluff couscous with a fork. Stir in pecans and parsley. **Yield:** 4 servings.

BASIL BATTER ROLLS

These pesto-flavored batter rolls couldn't be easier—no kneading!

2 packages active dry yeast	1½ teaspoons salt
1½ cups warm water (105° to 115°)	1 large egg
⅓ cup shortening	2 tablespoons pesto
4 cups unbleached flour, divided	2 cloves garlic, minced
¼ cup sugar	Cooking spray
	Melted butter or margarine (optional)

COMBINE yeast and warm water in a 2-cup liquid measuring cup; let stand 5 minutes.

COMBINE yeast mixture, shortening, 2 cups flour, and next 3 ingredients in a large mixing bowl; beat at medium speed with an electric mixer until well blended. Stir in pesto and garlic. Gradually stir in enough remaining flour to make a soft dough. (Dough will be sticky.)

COVER and let rise in a warm place (85°), free from drafts, 50 minutes or until doubled in bulk.

STIR dough; spoon into greased muffin pans, filling half full. Spray roll tops with cooking spray; cover and let rise in a warm place, free from drafts, 45 minutes.

BAKE at 375° for 15 minutes or until golden. Brush with melted butter, if desired. **Yield:** 18 rolls.

Basil Matters

*R*eferred to by the ancient Greeks as the royal herb, basil is actually a member of the mint family. It's an annual herb that, when fresh, has a pungent flavor and is used often as an important ingredient in Mediterranean, Italian, and more increasingly, American cooking. This summer herb can be grown indoors during the winter months if placed near a sunny window.

Cut fresh basil will keep up to four days if stored properly. Wrap the leaves in a slightly damp paper towel, place in a plastic bag, and chill.

Stable Café: Chef's Choice

FRESH STRAWBERRY NAPOLEONS

*Three small rectangular wafers of crisp puff pastry stack
into stately individual desserts with thick pastry cream sandwiched between
the layers. This dessert is sure to melt in your mouth.*

½ (17¼-ounce) package puff
   pastry (1 sheet)
2 cups Pastry Cream

2 cups fresh strawberries, sliced
1 tablespoon powdered sugar

ROLL pastry into a 12- x 10-inch rectangle on a lightly floured surface. Transfer pastry to an ungreased baking sheet. Lay another ungreased baking sheet over pastry. Bake at 400° for 13 minutes or until golden. Cool.

CUT pastry into 3 lengthwise strips. Cut each strip into 4 (3-inch) rectangles. Spoon or pipe 2 tablespoons Pastry Cream onto 4 rectangles. Top with half of strawberries. Spoon 2 teaspoons cream over berries. Top with another rectangle of pastry. Repeat procedure with remaining Pastry Cream and strawberries, ending with a third rectangle of pastry. Sift powdered sugar lightly over top pastry. **Yield:** 4 servings.

PASTRY CREAM

2 cups milk
1 vanilla bean, split
½ cup sugar

3 tablespoons cornstarch
¼ teaspoon salt
2 eggs

HEAT milk and vanilla bean in a medium saucepan over medium-high heat until bubbles form around edges. Remove from heat.

COMBINE sugar, cornstarch, and salt in a bowl. Add eggs; stir with a wire whisk until smooth. Slowly add one-third hot milk to egg mixture, whisking constantly. Pour egg mixture into saucepan with milk. Place over medium-high heat. Cook 5 minutes, or until mixture is thickened. Remove vanilla bean.

TRANSFER mixture to a bowl; cover and chill. **Yield:** 2 cups.

LUNCH
AMONG THE
WILDFLOWERS

Roasted Red Bell Pepper Tapenade

Breadsticks

Pita Niçoise

Honeyed Fruit Cups

Ruby Tea or
⚜ *Biltmore Estate Cabernet Blanc de Noir*

Lemon Chess Pie

Serves 6

ROASTED RED BELL PEPPER TAPENADE

This recipe yields an abundance of tapenade; the leftovers are great on pasta, grilled fish, or chicken.

4 large red bell peppers
1 (8-ounce) package sliced fresh mushrooms
¼ cup chopped purple onion
2 cloves garlic, minced
2 tablespoons olive oil, divided
1 cup grated Parmesan cheese
½ cup Italian-seasoned breadcrumbs
¼ cup walnut pieces, finely chopped

2 tablespoons minced fresh basil or 2 teaspoons dried basil
2 teaspoons lemon juice
1 teaspoon Worcestershire sauce
¼ teaspoon salt
¼ teaspoon black pepper
¼ teaspoon hot sauce
Garnish: fresh fennel sprigs

CUT peppers in half crosswise; discard seeds. Place peppers, skin side up, on a baking sheet; flatten with palm of hand. Broil peppers 5½ inches from heat 5 to 10 minutes or until charred.

PLACE bell peppers in a heavy-duty, zip-top plastic bag; seal and let stand 10 minutes to loosen skins. Peel peppers, and discard skins.

SAUTÉ mushrooms, onion, and garlic in ½ tablespoon hot oil in a large skillet 10 minutes or until liquid evaporates. Remove from heat, and set aside.

PROCESS bell peppers in a food processor until smooth, stopping to scrape down sides. Add mushroom mixture, remaining 1½ tablespoons oil, cheese, and next 8 ingredients; pulse until ground.

SERVE with breadsticks, crackers, or assorted fresh vegetables. Garnish, if desired. **Yield:** 3 cups.

PITA NIÇOISE

*Niçoise refers to cuisine that hails from Nice, France, with signature ingredients
such as tomatoes, black olives, garlic, and anchovies. In this fresh sandwich,
we've opted for tuna instead of anchovies.*

2 (8-ounce) tuna fillets*
½ pound new potatoes
¼ pound French baby green
   beans
⅔ cup mayonnaise
2 large cloves garlic, crushed
1 teaspoon dried oregano
1 teaspoon lemon juice
½ teaspoon salt
½ teaspoon sugar
1 small purple onion, finely
   chopped

½ cup Niçoise olives or other
   small black olives, sliced
2 tablespoons red wine vinegar
½ teaspoon freshly ground
   pepper
3 large pita bread rounds
   Red leaf lettuce
3 Roma tomatoes, thinly sliced
2 tablespoons capers (optional)

PLACE tuna on a rack in a broiler pan. Broil 5½ inches from heat 4 to 6
minutes on each side or until fish flakes easily when tested with a fork. Cool
and break fish into chunks; set aside.

MEANWHILE, cook potatoes in a small amount of boiling water 10 to
15 minutes or until tender. Drain; let cool to touch, and coarsely chop potatoes. Trim stem ends of beans. Arrange beans in a vegetable steamer over
boiling water. Cover and steam 3 to 4 minutes or until crisp-tender. Plunge
in ice water to stop cooking process; drain and cut beans into ¾-inch pieces.

COMBINE mayonnaise and next 5 ingredients, stirring well. Combine
tuna, potato, beans, onion, and olives in a large bowl. Sprinkle with vinegar
and pepper; toss gently. Stir in mayonnaise mixture.

CUT pita rounds in half crosswise; line each half with lettuce and tomato. Spoon tuna mixture evenly into pita halves. Sprinkle with capers,
if desired. **Yield:** 6 servings.

*You can substitute 3 (6-ounce) cans of solid white tuna, drained and
broken into chunks, for fresh tuna.

HONEYED FRUIT CUPS

½ fresh pineapple, cored,
   peeled, and cubed (about
   2 cups)*
1 pint fresh strawberries
1 pint fresh blueberries

2 cups seedless grapes
½ cup fresh pineapple or orange
   juice*
2 tablespoons honey

COMBINE pineapple cubes, strawberries, blueberries, and grapes.
Combine pineapple juice and honey. Pour over fruit; toss to coat. Chill.
Yield: 6 cups.

*You can substitute 1 (20-ounce) can of unsweetened pineapple chunks
for fresh pineapple, and substitute its juice for fresh pineapple juice.

RUBY TEA

Strawberry-kiwi-flavored tea bags color this refreshing beverage ruby red.

2 quarts cold water
1 cup sugar
4 (3-inch) sticks cinnamon,
   broken into pieces
1 teaspoon whole cloves
10 regular-size strawberry-kiwi-
   flavored tea bags

4 fresh mint sprigs
1 cup pineapple juice
1 (11-ounce) bottle
   strawberry-flavored
   sparkling mineral water

COMBINE water, sugar, cinnamon, and cloves in a large saucepan. Bring
mixture to a boil, stirring occasionally. Add tea bags and mint; remove from
heat; cover and steep 10 minutes.
STRAIN tea into a pitcher. Add pineapple juice, and chill thoroughly.
Add sparkling water just before serving, and serve over ice. **Yield:** 2½ quarts.

LEMON CHESS PIE

½ (15-ounce) package
   refrigerated piecrusts
1 cup sugar
½ cup firmly packed brown
   sugar
2 tablespoons all-purpose flour
5 large eggs

½ teaspoon grated lemon rind
⅓ cup fresh lemon juice
⅓ cup butter or margarine,
   melted
¼ teaspoon ground nutmeg
   Whipped cream (optional)

PLACE piecrust in a 9-inch pie plate. Flute edges; set aside.

COMBINE sugars and flour in a large bowl. Add eggs, one at a time, beating at medium speed with an electric mixer until blended. Add next 4 ingredients; mix well. Pour into prepared piecrust. Bake at 325° for 45 minutes. Dollop with whipped cream, if desired. **Yield:** one (9-inch) pie.

The Name Game: Chess Pie

*C*onsidered one of the South's favorite desserts, chess pie is not without controversy. The terms chess and cheese were once used interchangeably in Britain. To that end, there has been confusion over the difference, if any, between cheese pie and chess pie for many years. In Mrs. Porter's New Southern Cookery Book, written by a Virginian in 1871, there is a recipe for "Real Cheesecake." Although it calls for "four ounces of rich (not strong or old) cheese," it is a pie, baked in a pastry-lined tin. This recipe is followed by five additional "cheese-cakes," all of which are pies, not cakes, and none of which contain cheese. Today, we refer to these as chess pies. Apparently in those days, if one wished to say "cheese," one was compelled to say "real cheese."

FOURTH OF JULY BARBECUE

Grilled Barbecue Chicken

Bacon, Dill, and Onion Potato Salad

Corn on the Cob

Baked Beans Quintet

Grilled Bread

Red or White Wine Cooler or
Iced Tea

Old-Fashioned Peach Ice Cream or
Black Bottom Peanut Butter Pie, *page 156*

Serves 8

GRILLED BARBECUE CHICKEN

This sauce recipe contains so many enticing ingredients that its rich, smoky flavor ensures your barbecue is a sizzling success. Try it on smoked beef or pork, too.

¼ cup finely diced celery	2 tablespoons seasoning salt
½ cup finely diced onion	2 tablespoons Worcestershire sauce
½ cup finely diced green bell pepper	1 tablespoon chili powder
2 tablespoons butter	2 to 3 teaspoons liquid smoke
3 (12-ounce) bottles chili sauce	1 teaspoon ground white pepper
1 cup firmly packed brown sugar	1 teaspoon ground cumin
¼ cup cider vinegar	1 teaspoon ground black pepper
1 clove garlic	½ teaspoon ground red pepper
2 tablespoons dry mustard	½ teaspoon gumbo filé
	2 (2½- to 3-pound) broiler-fryers, quartered

SAUTÉ celery, onion, and bell pepper in butter in a large saucepan over medium heat 5 minutes or until tender. Add chili sauce and next 13 ingredients. Simmer gently over low heat, covered, 1 hour. Cover and chill half of sauce for serving with chicken.

COOK chicken, covered with grill lid, over medium-hot coals (350° to 400°) 50 to 60 minutes or until meat thermometer inserted in thickest part of chicken thigh registers 180°, basting frequently with remaining sauce and turning occasionally. Serve chicken with reserved sauce. **Yield:** 8 servings.

BACON, DILL, AND ONION POTATO SALAD

2 pounds small round red potatoes, unpeeled	½ cup sour cream
3 green onions, chopped	¼ cup milk
½ pound bacon, cooked and crumbled	3 tablespoons chopped fresh dill
1 green bell pepper, seeded and diced	1 tablespoon lemon juice
1 hard-cooked egg, chopped	2 teaspoons Dijon mustard
	½ teaspoon salt

SLICE potatoes into ¼-inch-thick slices. Place potato in a large saucepan; add water to cover. Bring to a boil; cover, reduce heat, and simmer 15 minutes. Drain.

COMBINE potato, green onions, and next 3 ingredients in a bowl; toss gently.

COMBINE sour cream and remaining 5 ingredients in a small bowl; stir well. Pour dressing over potato mixture; toss gently. Cover and chill. **Yield:** 12 servings.

BAKED BEANS QUINTET

Five types of beans make this just about the best-looking and best-tasting bean dish around. It's splendid for serving at a barbecue.

6 slices bacon	1 (19-ounce) can garbanzo beans, drained
1 cup chopped onion	
1 clove garlic, minced	¾ cup ketchup
1 (16-ounce) can butterbeans, drained	½ cup molasses
	⅓ cup firmly packed brown sugar
1 (15¼-ounce) can lima beans, drained	
	1½ tablespoons Worcestershire sauce
1 (15-ounce) can pork and beans	
	1 tablespoon prepared mustard
1 (15¼-ounce) can red kidney beans, drained	½ teaspoon pepper

COOK bacon in a large skillet until crisp; remove bacon, reserving drippings in skillet. Crumble bacon, and set aside.

COOK onion and garlic in bacon drippings, stirring constantly, until tender; drain.

COMBINE bacon, onion mixture, butterbeans, and remaining ingredients in a large bowl. Spoon mixture into a lightly greased 2½-quart bean pot or baking dish. Cover and bake at 375° for 1 hour. **Yield:** 8 servings.

GRILLED BREAD

If your grill rack is too full for the bread, wrap the bread in heavy-duty
aluminum foil, and bake at 375° for 10 to 15 minutes or until thoroughly heated.

1 (16-ounce) loaf French or
   Italian bread
½ cup butter, softened
1 tablespoon finely chopped
   fresh parsley or 2
   teaspoons dried parsley
   flakes

1 teaspoon garlic powder

SLICE bread loaf into 1-inch slices. Combine butter, parsley, and garlic powder; spread 1 side of each bread slice with garlic butter. Grill slices over medium-hot coals (350° to 400°) 1 minute. Turn bread slices, using hot pads or tongs, and grill 30 more seconds. Serve warm. **Yield:** 8 servings.

Bistro: Chef's Choice
RED OR WHITE WINE COOLER

You can choose red or white wine for this refreshing, slightly sweet beverage.

¾ cup superfine sugar
¼ cup water
8 cups Biltmore Estate
   Cabernet Sauvignon or
   Biltmore Estate
   Chardonnay Sur Lies or
   other dry red or dry white
   wine

1 cup orange juice
   Garnish: lemon or orange
   slices

COMBINE sugar and water, stirring until sugar dissolves. Add wine and orange juice; stir well. Serve over ice. Garnish, if desired. **Yield:** 10 cups.

OLD-FASHIONED PEACH ICE CREAM

For this ice cream, use fragrant, ripe peaches.
They impart a perfumy aroma and will be easy to mash.

5 large eggs

1½ cups sugar, divided

1 (14-ounce) can sweetened
    condensed milk

1 (12-ounce) can evaporated
    milk

1 tablespoon vanilla extract

2 cups mashed fresh peaches

5 cups milk
    Garnish: fresh peach slices

BEAT eggs at medium speed with an electric mixer until frothy; add 1 cup sugar, and beat well. Add condensed milk, evaporated milk, and vanilla, mixing well. Pour mixture into a large heavy saucepan. Cook over medium heat until mixture comes to a boil, stirring constantly; boil 1 minute. Let mixture cool. Combine mashed peaches and remaining ½ cup sugar. Add peach mixture to milk mixture.

POUR mixture into freezer container of a 5-quart hand-turned or electric freezer; add milk. Freeze according to manufacturer's instructions.

PACK freezer with additional ice and rock salt, and let stand 1 hour before serving. **Yield:** 1 gallon.

I Scream, You Scream...

*W*e all scream for ice cream...homemade ice cream, that is. Whether using a cooked custard like the one in our Old-Fashioned Peach Ice Cream above, or a no-cook base for your ice cream, start with the best ingredients. Pure flavorings, not imitations, will also give your ice cream a richer flavor.

Pay close attention to the fruit—try to use fully ripened fruit because underripe fruit freezes too hard. Always chop or mash fruit such as peaches or strawberries into small pieces. Sweetening fruit before adding it to the milk mixture will also keep the fruit from freezing too hard. If a recipe calls for whipped cream, whip only until soft peaks form, not until it's stiff. If possible, chill the cream mixture 4 hours or overnight to allow the flavors to blend and to yield a smoother texture.

SUMMER SOIRÉE ON THE PATIO

Chilled Roasted Bell Pepper Gazpacho

❧ *Biltmore Estate Sauvignon Blanc*

Grilled Salmon Salad with
Creamy Tarragon Dressing

Garlic and Pepper Loaves

White Sangría or
❧ *Biltmore Estate Chardonnay Sur Lies*

Chocolate Truffle Mousse

Serves 8

CHILLED ROASTED BELL PEPPER GAZPACHO

Roasting peppers caramelizes and intensifies their sweet flavor—
it's well worth the effort.

1 small red bell pepper

1 small green bell pepper

1 pound tomatoes, coarsely chopped

1 small onion, diced

1 medium cucumber, peeled, seeded, and diced

1 tablespoon minced garlic

1 tablespoon red wine vinegar

1 tablespoon lemon juice

1 tablespoon olive oil

2 teaspoons lime juice

½ teaspoon salt

¼ teaspoon black pepper

½ teaspoon hot sauce

2 cups tomato juice

1 cup beef broth

Garnishes: diced tomato, diced red bell pepper, diced green bell pepper, diced cucumber, and diced green onions

CUT bell peppers in half crosswise; discard seeds. Place peppers, skin side up, on a baking sheet; flatten with palm of hand. Broil peppers 5½ inches from heat 5 to 10 minutes or until charred. Place peppers in a heavy-duty, zip-top plastic bag. Seal bag and let stand 10 minutes to loosen skins. Peel peppers, and discard skins.

COMBINE peppers, tomato, and next 10 ingredients in a large bowl. Process half of mixture in an electric blender, and puree until smooth. Pour mixture into a separate large bowl. Repeat procedure with remaining half of vegetable mixture. Add tomato juice and broth; stir well. Cover and chill soup thoroughly. To serve, ladle soup evenly into 8 bowls and garnish, if desired. **Yield:** 7 cups.

GRILLED SALMON SALAD WITH CREAMY TARRAGON DRESSING

8 (6- to 8-ounce) salmon fillets
    (about 1½ inches thick)
⅓ cup soy sauce
1 teaspoon grated lemon rind
¼ cup fresh lemon juice
1 clove garlic, minced
2 teaspoons Dijon mustard
½ cup vegetable oil
12 cups mixed salad greens
    Creamy Tarragon Dressing
    Garnish: fresh tarragon
        sprigs

PLACE fillets in a large shallow dish. Combine soy sauce and next 5 ingredients, stirring well; pour over fillets. Cover and marinate in refrigerator 3 hours, turning each hour.

REMOVE fillets from marinade, discarding marinade. Grill fillets, covered with grill lid, over medium-hot coals (350° to 400°) 6 minutes on each side or until fish flakes easily when tested with a fork. To serve, place 1 fillet on 1½ cups salad greens, and top with ¼ cup Creamy Tarragon Dressing. Garnish, if desired. **Yield:** 8 servings.

Deerpark Restaurant: Chef's Choice
CREAMY TARRAGON DRESSING
The fresh herbs in this dressing also complement
poached fish, filet mignon, and steamed vegetables.

2 cups mayonnaise
⅓ cup buttermilk
3 tablespoons finely chopped
    fresh tarragon
2 tablespoons finely chopped
    fresh parsley
2 tablespoons chopped green
    onions
2 tablespoons tarragon vinegar
1½ teaspoons Worcestershire
    sauce
¼ teaspoon dried thyme
1 teaspoon sugar
1 teaspoon freshly ground
    pepper
½ teaspoon salt
½ teaspoon hot sauce

COMBINE all ingredients, and stir well with a wire whisk. Cover and chill. **Yield:** 2½ cups.

GARLIC AND PEPPER LOAVES

You won't need special French bread pans for this recipe.
Form the loaves by hand on large baking sheets for a rustic appearance.

1¾ cups water
  1 tablespoon butter or
       margarine
3¾ to 4¼ cups all-purpose
       flour, divided
  2 packages active dry yeast
  1 tablespoon sugar
  1 tablespoon garlic powder

  2 teaspoons salt
  1 teaspoon coarsely ground
       pepper
  1 teaspoon dried thyme
  1 tablespoon cornmeal
     Cooking spray
  1 egg white, lightly beaten
  1 tablespoon water

COMBINE 1¾ cups water and butter in a saucepan; heat until butter
melts, stirring occasionally. Cool to 120° to 130°.

COMBINE 1½ cups flour and next 6 ingredients in a large mixing bowl.
Gradually add liquid mixture to flour mixture, beating at medium speed with
an electric mixer. Beat 2 more minutes. Gradually stir in enough remaining
flour to make a soft dough. (Dough will be sticky.)

TURN dough out onto a well-floured surface, and knead until smooth
and elastic (about 5 minutes). Cover and let rest 20 minutes.

LIGHTLY grease 2 large baking sheets; sprinkle with cornmeal.

DIVIDE dough in half. Roll one portion of dough into a 15- x 10-inch
rectangle. Roll up dough, starting at long side, pressing firmly to eliminate air
pockets; pinch ends to seal.

PLACE dough, seam side down, on a prepared baking sheet. Repeat procedure with remaining portion of dough. Coat dough lightly with cooking
spray. Cover and chill 2 hours. Uncover and let stand at room temperature
10 minutes.

MAKE ¼-inch-deep slits diagonally across loaves. Bake at 425° for 20
minutes. Combine egg white and 1 tablespoon water; brush over loaves. Bake
5 more minutes or until golden. Cool completely on wire racks. **Yield:** 2 loaves.

WHITE SANGRÍA

Frozen grapes help chill this white wine version of the Spanish beverage.

2 lemons, thinly sliced	1 cup brandy
2 limes, thinly sliced	2 (1-liter) bottles lemon-lime
1½ cups sugar	sparkling water, chilled
2 (750-milliliter) bottles	1 cup seedless green grapes,
Biltmore Estate Sauvignon	frozen
Blanc or other dry white	
wine	

COMBINE first 5 ingredients in a large pitcher; stir well. Chill at least 2 hours. Gently stir in chilled sparkling water and frozen grapes just before serving. Serve over ice. **Yield:** 9 cups.

CHOCOLATE TRUFFLE MOUSSE

This rich chocolate mousse is so velvety smooth it resembles a truffle in texture.

16 (1-ounce) squares semisweet	¼ cup powdered sugar
chocolate	1 teaspoon vanilla extract
½ cup light corn syrup	1 cup fresh raspberries
½ cup butter or margarine	1 cup whipping cream,
4 egg yolks, lightly beaten	whipped
2 cups whipping cream, divided	Garnish: chocolate curls

COMBINE first 3 ingredients in a large heavy saucepan; cook over low heat, stirring constantly, until chocolate melts.

COMBINE egg yolks and ½ cup whipping cream. Gradually stir about 1 cup chocolate mixture into yolk mixture; add to remaining chocolate mixture, stirring constantly. Cook over medium-low heat 1 minute or until mixture reaches 160°. Remove from heat; cool to room temperature.

BEAT 1½ cups whipping cream at medium speed with an electric mixer until foamy; gradually add sugar, beating until soft peaks form. Stir in vanilla.

STIR 1 cup whipped cream mixture into chocolate mixture (to lighten it); then fold in remaining cream mixture. Spoon into eight stemmed glasses. Cover and chill least 8 hours. Top each serving with fresh raspberries and a dollop of whipped cream. Garnish, if desired. **Yield:** 8 servings.

What's in a Name?

Named for its red color, sangría comes from the Spanish word for bleeding. Sangaree, a West Indian derivative of the Spanish sangría, was very popular with early American colonists. The blood-red drink was generally made from red wine, citrus fruit juices, sugar, and spices in the late 16th century and is still popular in our country today. Sauvignon Blanc lends its sparkling color as the base for our white wine sangría.

AUTUMN RESPITE

Mushroom Strudel

 Château Biltmore Chardonnay

Molasses Pork Tenderloin

Green Beans with Shallots

Acorn Squash with Rosemary

Dinner Rolls

 Biltmore Estate Cardinal's Crest®

Cherries Jubilee with
 Biltmore Estate Sparkling Wine

Serves 4 to 6

Bistro: Chef's Choice
MUSHROOM STRUDEL

Portobello and shiitake mushrooms have a rich, meaty flavor and texture.
Teamed with the button mushrooms, they form a delightful trio in this elegant
appetizer. Any favorite combination of mushrooms substitutes well.

2 cups heavy whipping cream	1 teaspoon chopped fresh thyme
1 tablespoon olive oil	1 teaspoon chopped fresh parsley
1 cup portobello mushrooms, coarsely chopped	$\frac{1}{2}$ teaspoon salt
1 cup shiitake mushrooms, coarsely chopped	$\frac{1}{4}$ teaspoon pepper
1 cup button mushrooms, coarsely chopped	3 sheets frozen phyllo pastry, thawed
1 teaspoon minced garlic	Cooking spray
1 teaspoon minced shallot	2 tablespoons butter, melted
1 teaspoon chopped fresh basil	

PLACE whipping cream in a large skillet over medium heat; simmer 20 minutes or until reduced by half. Meanwhile, heat oil in a large skillet or Dutch oven over medium-high heat. Add mushrooms, and sauté 4 minutes or until tender.

ADD garlic and next 4 ingredients; sauté 5 minutes. Add reduced cream, salt, and pepper; simmer 15 minutes. Remove from heat, and let cool at least 1 hour.

PLACE one sheet of phyllo on a baking sheet coated lightly with cooking spray. Brush lightly with melted butter. Repeat this procedure twice, layering phyllo on baking sheet.

SPOON mushroom mixture onto one long end of phyllo; roll up phyllo jellyroll fashion. Brush top lightly with melted butter. Cut 1-inch slits across top of strudel. Bake at 400° for 25 minutes or until golden brown. Serve warm. **Yield:** 4 to 6 appetizer servings.

MOLASSES PORK TENDERLOIN

If the weather is too chilly for grilling the tenderloin, bake it,
uncovered, at 350° for 30 minutes.

¼ cup molasses

2 tablespoons stone-ground
    Dijon mustard

1 tablespoon apple cider vinegar

2 (¾-pound) pork tenderloins,
    trimmed

STIR together first 3 ingredients, and brush over pork tenderloins. Cover and chill 8 hours.

GRILL, covered with grill lid, over medium-hot coals (350° to 400°) about 10 minutes on each side or until a meat thermometer inserted into thickest portion registers 160°. **Yield:** 4 to 6 servings.

GREEN BEANS WITH SHALLOTS

You can substitute 2 sliced green onions for
the subtle, mild flavor of shallots, if desired.

1¾ pounds fresh green beans,
      trimmed

2 shallots, minced

1 tablespoon olive oil

1 tablespoon water

½ teaspoon salt

⅛ teaspoon pepper

PLACE beans in saucepan; cover with water. Boil 10 minutes or until crisp-tender. Drain.

SAUTÉ shallots in hot oil in saucepan 3 minutes or until tender. Add green beans, 1 tablespoon water, salt, and pepper; cook, stirring occasionally, 3 minutes or until thoroughly heated. **Yield:** 6 servings.

ACORN SQUASH WITH ROSEMARY

Cook the squash in a stove-top grill skillet
for a cold weather alternative to outdoor grilling.

1	tablespoon olive oil, divided	4	cloves garlic, pressed
¼	cup white wine vinegar	1½	pounds acorn squash, thinly sliced
1	tablespoon fresh or dried rosemary		Garnish: fresh rosemary sprigs
½	teaspoon salt		

COMBINE ½ tablespoon olive oil, vinegar, and next 3 ingredients in a large heavy-duty, zip-top plastic bag; add squash. Let stand 2 hours, turning occasionally.

REMOVE squash from marinade, reserving marinade. Brush squash with remaining ½ tablespoon oil.

GRILL squash, covered with grill lid, over medium-hot coals (350° to 400°) about 10 minutes on each side. Place on a serving dish; drizzle with reserved marinade. Cover and let stand 10 minutes. Garnish, if desired.
Yield: 4 to 6 servings.

Squash Anyone?

*T*here are many members of the squash family, ranging from ivory to ebony, from petite to gargantuan, and from savory to sugary. Almost all of these, with the exception of spaghetti squash, are interchangeable in our recipe above. Slice summer squash lengthwise and reduce cooking time as needed.

CHERRIES JUBILEE WITH
BILTMORE ESTATE SPARKLING WINE

2 (11-ounce) cans pitted Bing
    cherries, undrained
1 cup kirsch or other cherry-
    flavored brandy, divided
1 tablespoon cornstarch
1 tablespoon butter or
    margarine
3 tablespoons grated orange
    rind (about 1 orange)

3 tablespoons brown sugar
1 cup Biltmore Estate Blanc de
    Blanc-Brut Sparkling Wine
    or other sparkling white
    wine
Garnish: crisp cookies

DRAIN cherries, reserving ¾ cup liquid; combine reserved liquid and ¾ cup kirsch in a small saucepan. Stir in cornstarch, and cook over medium-high heat, stirring constantly, until mixture is thickened; let cool.

MELT butter in a large skillet; add orange rind, and sauté 3 minutes. Add cherries, and sprinkle with brown sugar; sauté 4 or 5 minutes or until sugar dissolves and mixture becomes slightly thickened. Add sparkling wine, and simmer 6 to 8 minutes, stirring often. Add kirsch mixture; toss and bring to a simmer. Reduce heat, and keep warm.

PLACE remaining ¼ cup kirsch in a small, long-handled saucepan; heat just until warm (do not boil). Remove from heat. Ignite with a long match; pour over cherries. Stir until flames die down. Serve immediately over white chocolate ice cream or vanilla ice cream. Garnish, if desired. **Yield:** 6 servings.

WINE & CHEESE REUNION

Peppered Goat Cheese with
Baguette Slices or
Spinach-Herb Cheesecake, *page 80*

Herb-Marinated Olives

Roasted Red Bell Pepper Roulades

Cocktail Cheese Muffins

Marinated Stuffed Shrimp

Butterscotch Dip for Fruit or
Kahlúa-Pecan Brie, *page 80*

Spiced Cranberry Cider

⚜ *Biltmore Estate Sauvignon Blanc*

⚜ *Biltmore Estate Merlot*

Serves 12

PEPPERED GOAT CHEESE

One log of this cheese should serve 12 people at this appetizer buffet.
If you serve it as a single appetizer before dinner,
it will serve 6 to 8.

2 tablespoons cracked black
   pepper
1 (11-ounce) log goat cheese
2 tablespoons extra-virgin
   olive oil

Garnish: fresh rosemary
   sprigs

SPRINKLE pepper on a square of wax paper. Roll goat cheese log over pepper to coat. Drizzle with oil. Serve with toasted baguette slices. Garnish, if desired. **Yield:** 1 (6-inch) log.

HERB-MARINATED OLIVES

After eating these marinated olives, serve any remaining herbed oil
as a vinaigrette for salad greens or dipping oil for French bread.

½ cup olive oil
⅓ cup sherry vinegar or other
   flavored vinegar
2 cloves garlic, cut into slivers
1 tablespoon chopped fresh
   thyme or 1 teaspoon
   dried thyme
1½ teaspoons chopped fresh
   oregano or ½ teaspoon
   dried oregano

1 teaspoon fresh or dried
   rosemary
1 dried red pepper pod*
1 (10-ounce) jar kalamata
   olives, drained, or 1 (7.25-
   ounce) can colossal ripe,
   pitted olives, drained
1 (7-ounce) jar pimiento-
   stuffed olives, drained
Fresh herb sprigs (optional)

COMBINE first 7 ingredients in a bowl; stir well. Place olives in a large heavy-duty, zip-top plastic bag. Pour marinade over olives. Seal bag securely. Marinate in refrigerator 8 hours or up to 5 days, turning occasionally. Transfer to a decorative container, and add fresh herbs, if desired. To serve, spoon desired amount of olives into a serving dish. **Yield:** 22 appetizer servings.

*Find red pepper pods with other spices and herbs in specialty markets.

ROASTED RED BELL PEPPER ROULADES

*If you have time, wrap the rolls in plastic wrap, and chill 1 hour before
slicing to develop the savory flavor of the filling.*

1 small ripe avocado
1 tablespoon finely chopped
   onion
¾ teaspoon lemon or lime juice
¼ teaspoon salt
2 cloves garlic, pressed
1 (7-ounce) jar roasted red bell
   peppers

4 (8-inch) flour tortillas
1 (3-ounce) package cream
   cheese or log goat cheese,
   softened
¼ teaspoon freshly ground
   black pepper
Garnish: fresh basil sprigs

CUT avocado in half, and remove seed from avocado. Scoop out avocado
pulp into a large bowl. Mash until avocado is desired consistency. Add onion
and next 3 ingredients; stir until blended. Set aside.

DRAIN roasted peppers, and pat dry with paper towels; coarsely chop,
and set aside.

SPREAD tortillas evenly with cheese; spread avocado mixture evenly
over cheese.

SPRINKLE with chopped red pepper and ground black pepper. Roll up,
pressing edges to seal; cut each roll into 6 slices using a serrated knife. Secure
slices with wooden picks. Garnish, if desired. **Yield:** 2 dozen.

NOTE: You can substitute ¾ cup of your favorite guacamole for avocado
and the next 4 ingredients.

COCKTAIL CHEESE MUFFINS

*If you have any of these mini-muffins left after the party,
serve them with a bowl of hot soup or chili.*

¾ cup butter or margarine

2 cups (8 ounces) shredded
sharp Cheddar cheese

2 cups self-rising flour

1 (8-ounce) carton sour cream

2 tablespoons fresh chopped
chives

MELT butter in a medium saucepan over medium heat. Add
Cheddar cheese, and cook 2 minutes, stirring constantly. Stir in flour, sour
cream, and chives.

SPOON batter into ungreased miniature (1¾-inch) muffin pans, filling
two-thirds full. Bake at 375° for 20 to 22 minutes. Remove pans to wire racks
and let cool 2 minutes. Remove muffins from pans, and serve immediately.
Yield: 4 dozen.

MARINATED STUFFED SHRIMP

*To save time, buy the shrimp already peeled. Twelve ounces raw, peeled fresh
shrimp equals one pound of unpeeled shrimp.*

1 pound unpeeled colossal
jumbo fresh shrimp (10 to
15 count)

2 cloves garlic, minced

1 teaspoon salt

1 teaspoon freshly ground
black pepper

2 tablespoons olive oil

1 (3.5-ounce) round smoked
Gouda cheese

4 ounces prosciutto or country
ham, thinly sliced

½ cup olive oil

¼ cup white balsamic vinegar

2 tablespoons chopped fresh
rosemary

⅛ teaspoon ground red pepper

PEEL shrimp, and devein. To help shrimp curve during cooking, make a
deep slit down the back of each shrimp using a small pairing knife, cutting to
but not through inside curve of shrimp.

SAUTÉ shrimp and next 3 ingredients in 2 tablespoons hot oil in a
skillet 3 minutes or until shrimp turn pink; cool.

To Devein or Not to Devein?

*That little black line that runs
down the back of a shrimp
(the sand vein) is its intestinal tract.
In small shrimp, it's really not
noticeable and is generally left intact.
But for larger shrimp in recipes like
Marinated Stuffed Shrimp at right,
the vein is unappealing and adds a
gritty, muddy taste. While there's no
harm in eating cooked shrimp that
haven't been deveined, many people
prefer to remove the vein.*

*Deveining is a simple process and
worth the effort. To devein shrimp,
simply slit the shrimp lengthwise
down its back, using a small paring
knife. Then pull the vein away with
the tip of the knife.*

CUT cheese into 1-inch cubes. Cut prosciutto into thin strips. Wrap ham strips around cheese cubes; insert cubes into shrimp, securing with wooden picks. Cover and chill 10 minutes.

WHISK together ½ cup oil and next 3 ingredients in a large bowl; add shrimp, and toss. Cover and chill 10 minutes. Remove shrimp from marinade, discarding marinade. **Yield:** 10 to 15 appetizer servings.

BUTTERSCOTCH DIP FOR FRUIT

Dunk a crisp apple wedge into this creamy dip, and you'll think you're eating a caramel apple.

½ cup butter or margarine	1 teaspoon coconut extract
1 cup firmly packed light brown sugar	1 teaspoon almond extract
1 (14-ounce) can sweetened condensed milk	½ teaspoon rum extract

COMBINE butter and brown sugar in a 3-quart saucepan; cook over medium-low heat 10 minutes, stirring occasionally. Add sweetened condensed milk; cook 6 minutes or until thickened and bubbly. Remove from heat, and stir in flavorings. Serve warm with sliced apple and other fruit. (This creamy dip forms small crystals after cooling, so reheat it over low heat just before serving to dissolve crystals.) **Yield:** 2¼ cups.

SPICED CRANBERRY CIDER

Offer this sweet, tart beverage as an alternative to alcohol.

2 quarts apple cider	4 (3-inch) cinnamon sticks
6 cups cranberry juice cocktail	1½ teaspoons whole cloves
¼ to ⅓ cup firmly packed brown sugar	1 lemon, thinly sliced
	Garnish: cinnamon sticks

BRING first 6 ingredients to a boil in a large Dutch oven, stirring often; reduce heat, and simmer 15 to 20 minutes. Remove spices and lemon. Garnish each serving, if desired. **Yield:** 14 cups.

A CHRISTMAS FEAST

Poinsettia Punch, *page 88*

Cranberry-Orange Glazed Ham

Wild Mushroom and Onion Risotto

Brussels Sprouts with Mustard Vinaigrette

Baked Pears with Walnuts and Gorgonzola

Rye-Sour Cream Dinner Rolls

Sweet Potato Cheesecake

⚜ *Château Biltmore Cabernet Franc*

Serves 6

CRANBERRY-ORANGE GLAZED HAM

1	(5- to 7-pound) smoked, fully cooked ham half	2	tablespoons cider vinegar
	Whole cloves	2	teaspoons all-purpose flour
1¼	cups firmly packed brown sugar, divided	1½	tablespoons prepared mustard
¾	cups cranberry juice cocktail	1½	tablespoons butter or margarine
¼	cup honey		Garnishes: orange slices, fresh cranberries

SLICE skin away from ham. Score fat on ham in a diamond design, and stud with whole cloves. Place ham, fat side up, on a rack in a shallow roasting pan. Insert meat thermometer, making sure it does not touch fat or bone. Bake, uncovered, at 325° for 1 hour.

COMBINE ¼ cup brown sugar, cranberry juice, and next 5 ingredients in a saucepan, mixing well. Bring to a boil, and cook 1 minute.

COAT exposed portion of ham with remaining 1 cup sugar. Pour hot cranberry juice mixture over ham; bake 30 more minutes or until thermometer registers 140°, basting ham with pan juices twice. Garnish, if desired. **Yield:** 10 to 14 servings.

WILD MUSHROOM AND ONION RISOTTO

You can also serve this creamy, Italian-inspired rice dish as an accompaniment to roast turkey or pork. It's a welcome change of pace from dressing.

2½	cups chicken broth	1	cup sliced fresh crimini mushrooms
1	cup chopped onion	¼	cup freshly grated Parmesan cheese
1	clove garlic, crushed		
2	teaspoons olive oil	2	tablespoons Biltmore Estate Chardonnay Sur Lies or other dry white wine
1	cup Arborio or other short-grain rice, uncooked		
1	(3.5-ounce) package fresh shiitake mushrooms, sliced		Garnish: fresh herb sprigs

BRING broth to a boil in a small saucepan. Cover, reduce heat to low, and keep warm.

COOK onion and garlic in oil in a large skillet over medium heat, stirring constantly, until onion is tender. Add rice, and cook 4 minutes, stirring constantly. Add mushrooms and ½ cup warm broth; cook, stirring constantly, until most of the liquid is absorbed.

CONTINUE adding broth, ½ cup at a time, stirring constantly until rice is tender and mixture is creamy, allowing rice to absorb most of liquid each time before adding more broth. (The entire process should take about 25 minutes.) Stir in cheese and wine. Transfer mixture to a serving bowl, and garnish, if desired. Serve immediately. **Yield:** 6 servings.

BRUSSELS SPROUTS WITH MUSTARD VINAIGRETTE

A tangy vinaigrette elevates these brussels sprouts to a dish befitting the holiday table. Small sprouts are the most tender.

1½ pounds fresh brussels sprouts*	1 tablespoon Dijon mustard
½ cup olive oil	2 teaspoons sugar
3 tablespoons red wine vinegar	½ teaspoon salt
2 tablespoons white wine Worcestershire sauce	½ teaspoon pepper
	½ cup mandarin orange segments

WASH brussels sprouts; remove discolored leaves. Cut off stem ends, and cut a shallow "X" in the bottom of each sprout. Place brussels sprouts in a saucepan; add water to cover. Bring to a boil; cover, reduce heat, and simmer 8 minutes or until tender. Drain. Transfer brussels sprouts to a serving bowl; keep warm.

COMBINE olive oil and next 6 ingredients in a saucepan. Cook over medium heat until thoroughly heated. Pour over brussels sprouts. Add orange segments; toss gently. Serve warm. **Yield:** 6 servings.

*You can substitute 3 (10-ounce) packages frozen brussels sprouts for 1½ pounds fresh brussels sprouts.

BAKED PEARS WITH WALNUTS AND GORGONZOLA

These pears are baked then broiled with a sweet, toasty, and pungent cheese topping.

3 large ripe pears, such as Bartlett, Bosc, or Anjou
2 tablespoons butter or margarine, softened
¼ teaspoon salt
¼ teaspoon ground white pepper
⅛ teaspoon ground nutmeg

1 (2.25-ounce) package walnut pieces (about ½ cup), chopped and toasted
3 tablespoons brown sugar
1½ tablespoons butter or margarine, melted
⅓ cup crumbled Gorgonzola cheese

PEEL pears, if desired; cut in half, and core. If needed, slice about ¼ inch from rounded sides to make pears sit flat. Brush pears with softened butter, and place, cored side down, in a buttered 13- x 9- x 2-inch pan.

BAKE at 450° for 15 minutes. Remove from oven, turn pears over, and sprinkle with salt, white pepper, and nutmeg. Bake 10 to 15 more minutes or until soft and lightly browned.

MEANWHILE, combine walnuts, brown sugar, and melted butter in a small bowl, stirring to coat nuts. Top pear halves with walnut mixture and cheese. Broil pears 5½ inches from heat until cheese melts. **Yield:** 6 servings.

RYE-SOUR CREAM DINNER ROLLS

1 package active dry yeast
¾ cup warm water (105° to 115°)
1 tablespoon sugar
1 cup rye flour
½ cup sour cream

2 tablespoons caraway seeds, divided
2 teaspoons salt
2 to 2½ cups all-purpose flour

COMBINE first 3 ingredients in a 2-cup liquid measuring cup; let stand 5 minutes.

COMBINE yeast mixture, rye flour, sour cream, 1 tablespoon caraway seeds, and salt in a large mixing bowl; beat at medium speed with an electric mixer until well blended. Gradually stir in enough all-purpose flour to make a soft dough.

TURN dough out onto a heavily floured surface, and knead until smooth and elastic (about 8 minutes). Place in a well-greased bowl, turning to grease top. Cover and let rise in a warm place (85°), free from drafts, 1 hour or until doubled in bulk.

PUNCH dough down, and divide into fourths; shape each portion into 3 (2-inch) balls. Dip tops of balls into remaining 1 tablespoon caraway seeds. Place balls 1 inch apart in a greased 13- x 9- x 2-inch pan.

COVER and let rise in a warm place, free from drafts, 45 minutes or until doubled in bulk. Bake at 400° for 18 minutes or until lightly browned. Remove from pans immediately. Serve warm. **Yield:** 1 dozen.

Stable Café: Chef's Choice
SWEET POTATO CHEESECAKE

2 cups graham cracker crumbs	½ teaspoon ground nutmeg
½ cup butter, melted	8 large eggs
½ teaspoon ground cinnamon	¾ cup sweet potato pie filling
½ teaspoon ground nutmeg	1 (16-ounce) carton sour cream
4 (8-ounce) packages cream cheese, softened	½ cup sugar
2 cups sugar	Garnishes: whipped cream, pecan halves
1 teaspoon ground cinnamon	

COMBINE first 4 ingredients; press mixture firmly in bottom and 1 inch up sides of a 10-inch springform pan.

BEAT cream cheese at medium speed with an electric mixer until smooth. Add 2 cups sugar, 1 teaspoon cinnamon, and ½ teaspoon nutmeg, beating well. Add eggs, one at a time, beating just until blended after each addition. Stir in pie filling, using a wire whisk. Spoon cream cheese mixture into prepared pan. Bake at 300° for 1½ hours or until set.

COMBINE sour cream and ½ cup sugar, stirring well. Pour sour cream mixture over cheesecake; return to oven for 10 more minutes. Cool completely on a wire rack. Cover and chill 8 hours. Remove sides of springform pan just before serving. Garnish, if desired. **Yield:** 1 (10-inch) cheesecake.

Deck the Dining Room

*S*easonal fruit can add a festive flair to your dining room for the holidays. To create a simple but fragrant centerpiece, tie oranges and limes with decorative ribbon, stud with upholstery tacks, and then arrange inside a large serving bowl or soup tureen.

A chandelier swag is a dining room's crowning touch. To make your own, thread kumquats, crab apples, and dried orange slices on florist wire, and attach to the chandelier. Finish the look with ribbon streamers.

CANDLELIGHT CHRISTMAS FOR TWO

Filet Mignon with Mushroom-Wine Sauce

Horseradish Mashed Potatoes

Green Beans with Caramelized Onion and Bacon or
Raspberry Salad with Balsamic Vinaigrette

Dinner Rolls

⚜ *Château Biltmore Claret*

⚜ *Biltmore Estate Riesling* or
Hot Buttered Bourbon

Crème Brûlée

Serves 2

FILET MIGNON WITH MUSHROOM-WINE SAUCE

1 tablespoon butter or
    margarine
3 tablespoons minced shallot
¼ pound fresh shiitake
    mushrooms, stems removed
½ cup Biltmore Estate
    Cardinal's Crest or other
    dry red wine
½ (10½-ounce) can condensed
    beef broth, undiluted
2 (6- to 8-ounce) beef
    tenderloin steaks (about 1
    inch thick)

½ teaspoon cracked black pepper
¼ cup Biltmore Estate
    Cardinal's Crest or other
    dry red wine
1½ teaspoons soy sauce
1 teaspoon cornstarch
1½ teaspoons chopped fresh
    thyme

MELT half of the butter in a nonstick skillet; add shallot and mushrooms, and sauté 4 minutes. Add ½ cup wine and ⅓ cup of the beef broth; cook, stirring often, 3 to 4 minutes. Using a slotted spoon, transfer mushrooms to a small bowl, reserving drippings in skillet.

COOK drippings over high heat, stirring often, 3 minutes or until reduced to ¼ cup. Add to mushrooms; set aside.

SPRINKLE steaks with pepper.

MELT remaining half of the butter in skillet; add steaks, and cook 3 minutes on each side or until meat is browned. Reduce heat to medium-low, and cook 1½ minutes on each side or to desired degree of doneness. Remove steaks, reserving drippings in skillet; keep steaks warm.

ADD ¼ cup wine and remaining broth to skillet, stirring to loosen browned particles. Bring to a boil; boil 1 minute.

COMBINE soy sauce and cornstarch, stirring until mixture is smooth; stir into wine mixture. Add mushroom mixture and chopped thyme. Bring to a boil; boil, stirring constantly, 1 minute. Serve sauce with steaks. **Yield:** 2 servings.

HORSERADISH MASHED POTATOES

Enjoy the unexpected kick fresh horseradish adds to mashed potatoes.

1 pound baking potatoes, cut
    into 1-inch chunks
3 tablespoons butter or
    margarine

¼ cup half-and-half
¼ teaspoon salt
1 to 1½ teaspoons freshly
    grated horseradish

PLACE potato chunks in saucepan; cover with water. Boil at medium-high heat 20 minutes or until tender; drain.

BEAT at medium speed with an electric mixer until smooth; add butter and remaining ingredients, and beat until fluffy. **Yield:** 2 servings.

RASPBERRY SALAD WITH BALSAMIC VINAIGRETTE

½ cup fresh raspberries
3 cups mixed salad greens

Balsamic Vinaigrette

COMBINE raspberries and greens; drizzle with desired amount of Balsamic Vinaigrette, tossing to coat. Chill leftover vinaigrette to use for other salads. **Yield:** 2 servings.

Bistro: Chef's Choice
BALSAMIC VINAIGRETTE

1 onion, finely diced (about
    1¾ cups)
1 cup olive oil, divided
½ teaspoon dried thyme
1 bay leaf, crushed

⅛ teaspoon salt
⅛ teaspoon pepper
½ teaspoon minced garlic
½ cup balsamic vinegar
1 tablespoon honey

SAUTÉ onion in ½ cup olive oil 10 to 15 minutes or until brown. Stir in thyme and next 6 ingredients; pour onion mixture into a bowl. Gradually add remaining ½ cup oil, stirring with a wire whisk until well blended. **Yield:** 1¾ cups.

GREEN BEANS WITH
CARAMELIZED ONION AND BACON

2	pounds fresh green beans	½	medium onion, sliced
2	slices bacon		

WASH beans; trim ends, and remove strings. Place beans in saucepan; cover with water. Boil 10 minutes or until crisp-tender. Drain and set aside.

COOK bacon in a large skillet over medium heat until crisp; remove bacon, reserving drippings in skillet. Crumble bacon, and set aside.

COOK onion in reserved bacon drippings over medium heat, stirring constantly, until tender and caramelized. Add beans to skillet, and toss gently. Cook just until thoroughly heated. Spoon bean mixture into a serving bowl; sprinkle with bacon. **Yield:** 2 servings.

HOT BUTTERED BOURBON

It's easy to make 2 or 20 servings of this winter beverage. You can freeze the ice cream mixture for up to 1 month, using only the desired amount for each serving.

1	pound butter, softened	1	quart vanilla ice cream,
1	(16-ounce) package light		softened
	brown sugar	1	liter bourbon
1	(16-ounce) package	4	quarts hot brewed coffee
	powdered sugar, sifted		Sweetened whipped cream
2	teaspoons ground cinnamon		Garnishes: cinnamon sticks,
2	teaspoons ground nutmeg		ground cinnamon

BEAT first 5 ingredients in a large bowl at medium speed with an electric mixer until light and fluffy. Stir in ice cream; freeze in an airtight container until firm.

TO MAKE SINGLE SERVINGS, combine 3 tablespoons ice cream mixture, 3 tablespoons bourbon, and ¾ cup coffee in a large mug, stirring well. Serve with sweetened whipped cream; garnish, if desired.

TO MAKE ENTIRE BATCH, combine ice cream mixture, bourbon, and coffee in a large bowl, stirring well. **Yield:** 20 servings.

CRÈME BRÛLÉE

Impart a subtle fragrance and flavor to your sugar:
Rinse and dry the vanilla bean after use, and place in your sugar bowl.

1 cup heavy whipping cream	7 large egg yolks
1 cup milk	2 tablespoons light brown sugar
½ vanilla bean, split	
½ cup sugar	2 tablespoons sugar

BRING cream, milk, and vanilla bean to a boil over medium-high heat. Remove vanilla bean with a slotted spoon. Reduce heat to low; keep warm.

BEAT sugar and egg yolks at medium speed with an electric mixer about 5 minutes or until sugar dissolves and mixture is smooth. Add one-third milk mixture to yolk mixture; stir well. Stir in remaining milk mixture. Ladle mixture into six (8-ounce) 3½- x 2-inch ramekins.

PLACE ramekins into a 13- x 9- x 2-inch baking dish. Add warm water to dish to depth of 1 inch. Bake at 275° for 50 minutes or until mixture is set. Allow custards to cool in water in pan on a wire rack.

COMBINE sugars in a small bowl. Sprinkle sugars evenly on tops of custards. Broil 5½ inches from heat 5 to 8 minutes or until sugar melts, rotating once if necessary for even cooking. Serve chilled or at room temperature. **Yield:** 6 servings.

Crème Brûlée Cravings

*T*his rich Italian dessert is not only delicious, but also fun to eat, as its hard caramel topping cracks with the pressure of a spoon. The rich custard has been enjoyed by many, including Thomas Jefferson, whose cook used a salamander (a hot metal branding iron) to make the caramel crust or "burnt cream." Today, cooks needn't use a red-hot branding iron, as your oven broiler caramelizes the sugar topping. Or, for the gadget enthusiast, simply sprinkle the custard with sugar and melt it with a kitchen torch designed for cooks.

COZY & CASUAL DINNER

Caesar Salad with Parmesan Wafers

Chicken with Marinara Sauce

Italian Dinner Rolls

Iced Tea or
❧ *Biltmore Estate Cardinal's Crest*®

Chocolate Fudge Pie

Serves 6

CAESAR SALAD WITH PARMESAN WAFERS

1	tablespoon anchovy fillets	⅛	teaspoon hot sauce
2	or 3 cloves garlic, chopped	1	cup olive oil
1	tablespoon fresh lemon juice	1	large head romaine lettuce
3	tablespoons champagne vinegar	1½	cups large croutons
1½	tablespoons Dijon mustard		Freshly grated Parmesan cheese
1	tablespoon egg substitute		Freshly ground black pepper
½	teaspoon sugar		Parmesan Wafers
½	teaspoon Worcestershire sauce		

PROCESS first 3 ingredients in an electric blender at low speed until smooth. Add vinegar and next 6 ingredients; process until well blended. Cover and chill.

WASH romaine under cold running water. Trim core, and separate head into leaves; discard wilted or discolored portions. Shake leaves to remove moisture. Place romaine in a large zip-top plastic bag; chill at least 2 hours. Cut coarse ribs from large leaves of romaine; tear leaves into bite-size pieces, and place in a large salad bowl.

POUR dressing over romaine; add croutons, and sprinkle with Parmesan cheese. Toss gently to coat. Sprinkle each serving with freshly ground black pepper. Serve each salad with 2 Parmesan Wafers. **Yield:** 6 servings.

PARMESAN WAFERS

1	cup freshly grated Parmesan cheese	¼	teaspoon freshly ground pepper
1	tablespoon all-purpose flour	1	tablespoon olive oil
½	teaspoon minced fresh thyme		

COMBINE all ingredients in a small bowl; stir just until moistened. Spoon mixture by level tablespoonfuls 2 inches apart onto an ungreased baking sheet. Spread each spoonful into a thin round. Bake at 375° for 4 minutes or until lightly browned. Remove to a wire rack to cool. **Yield:** 12 wafers.

Bistro: Chef's Choice
CHICKEN WITH MARINARA SAUCE

6   skinned and boned chicken breast halves
1   cup fine, dry breadcrumbs
½   cup grated Parmesan cheese
1   teaspoon salt
¼   teaspoon pepper
1   tablespoon chopped fresh basil
1   tablespoon chopped fresh oregano

½   cup all-purpose flour
2   large eggs, lightly beaten
3   tablespoons olive oil
    Marinara Sauce
2   cups (8 ounces) shredded mozzarella cheese
    Garnish: fresh basil sprigs

PLACE chicken between two sheets of heavy-duty plastic wrap; flatten to ¼-inch thickness, using a meat mallet or rolling pin.

COMBINE breadcrumbs and next 5 ingredients. Dredge chicken in flour; dip in egg, and coat with breadcrumb mixture.

BROWN chicken in hot oil in a skillet over medium heat. Remove from skillet; place in lightly greased au gratin dishes or a 13- x 9- x 2-inch baking dish. Spoon Marinara Sauce over chicken; top with mozzarella cheese. Bake at 400° for 8 minutes or until cheese melts. Garnish, if desired. **Yield:** 6 servings.

Stable Café: Chef's Choice
MARINARA SAUCE

1   tablespoon olive oil
6   large ripe tomatoes, chopped (about 8 cups)
3   cloves garlic, chopped

¼   cup chopped fresh parsley
6   basil leaves, chopped
¾   teaspoon salt
¼   teaspoon pepper

HEAT oil in a large skillet over medium-high heat until hot. Add tomato and garlic; cook 2 minutes. Reduce heat and simmer, uncovered, 1 hour and 10 minutes or until thick. Cool slightly. Position knife blade in food processor bowl; add tomato mixture. Process mixture until almost smooth. Pour through a wire-mesh strainer into a bowl, pushing solids through with the back of a spoon or rubber spatula. Return tomato mixture to pan. Stir in parsley, basil, salt, and pepper. Bring to a simmer; cook 10 minutes. **Yield:** 2½ cups.

Get a Rise Out of Rolls

*T*he mouthwatering flavor and aroma of a homemade yeast roll keep us wanting more. Many cooks, though, labor under the impression that yeast, the key ingredient for rising, is difficult to work with. Its beginnings are simple: ancient Egyptian breweries and bakeries were built side by side. A mixture containing wild yeast from the fermenting grain in the brewer's vats was carried to the baker, who added it to his dough; the dough rose, and the bread was baked.

Today, yeast can be bought as active dry yeast, rapid-rise yeast, bread-machine yeast, or cake yeast. Rapid-rise typically needs only one rising stage compared to two for other types of yeast. Check the expiration date on the yeast package before using it to be sure it's fresh.

Italian Dinner Rolls

4½ cups all-purpose flour, divided	1 cup milk
½ cup grated Parmesan cheese	½ cup water
2 tablespoons sugar	3 tablespoons butter or margarine
1½ teaspoons dried Italian seasoning	2 large eggs
1 teaspoon salt	2 tablespoons butter or margarine, melted
2 packages active dry yeast	¼ cup grated Parmesan cheese

COMBINE 1½ cups flour, ½ cup Parmesan cheese, and next 4 ingredients in a large mixing bowl; stir well. Combine milk, water, and 3 tablespoons butter in a saucepan; heat until butter melts, stirring occasionally. Cool to 120° to 130°.

GRADUALLY add liquid mixture to flour mixture, beating at low speed with an electric mixer. Beat 2 more minutes at medium speed. Add eggs; beat well. Gradually stir in enough remaining flour to make a soft dough.

TURN dough out onto a floured surface, and knead until smooth and elastic (8 to 10 minutes). Place in a well-greased bowl, turning to grease top. Cover and let rise in a warm place (85°), free from drafts, 45 minutes or until doubled in bulk.

PUNCH dough down; let rest 10 minutes. Turn dough out onto a lightly floured surface, and knead lightly 4 or 5 times. Divide dough into 16 equal portions; shape each piece into a ball. Dip tops of balls in 2 tablespoons melted butter, and then in ¼ cup Parmesan cheese. Arrange 8 balls in each of 2 greased 9-inch round pans. Cover and let rise in a warm place, free from drafts, 20 minutes or until doubled in bulk. Bake at 375° for 18 minutes or until golden. **Yield:** 16 rolls.

Deerpark Restaurant: Chef's Choice
CHOCOLATE FUDGE PIE

As the chocolate filling cooks, it rises substantially,
then falls again as the pie cools, creating its fudgy texture.

1¼ cups all-purpose flour
1 tablespoon sugar
½ teaspoon salt
½ teaspoon baking powder
¼ cup plus 2 tablespoons
    butter, chilled and cut into
    small pieces
1 large egg, lightly beaten
1 tablespoon cold water

⅔ cup dark corn syrup
⅔ cup sugar
4 (1-ounce) squares semisweet
    chocolate
¼ cup butter
3 large eggs
    Garnishes: whipped cream,
    chocolate shavings

COMBINE first 4 ingredients in a large bowl; cut in butter with pastry blender or two knives until mixture is crumbly. Add beaten egg and water; stir with a fork until ingredients are moistened. Turn dough out onto a lightly floured surface; knead quickly 3 or 4 times. Flatten dough into a disk; wrap in plastic wrap, and chill at least 1 hour.

ROLL pastry to ⅛-inch thickness on a lightly floured surface. Place in a 9-inch pieplate; trim off excess pastry along edges. Fold edges under, and crimp. Cover and chill crust.

MEANWHILE, combine corn syrup and ⅔ cup sugar in a medium saucepan. Bring to a boil over medium heat. Remove pan from heat. Stir in chocolate and ¼ cup butter. Whisk until smooth.

WHISK 3 eggs in a large bowl. Gradually whisk in chocolate mixture until well blended. Pour filling into crust.

BAKE at 350° for 50 minutes or until filling is set. Transfer to a wire rack; cool completely. Garnish, if desired. **Yield:** 8 servings

AFTER THE HUNT BRUNCH

Grapefruit Compote in Rosemary Syrup

Southern Brunch Casserole

Beaten Biscuits

Country Ham

Rum-Glazed Coffee Rolls or
Cinnamon-Sour Cream Streusel Loaf

Overnight Bloody Marys or
Mulled Wine Punch

Serves 10

GRAPEFRUIT COMPOTE IN ROSEMARY SYRUP

Citrus and rosemary create quite an impression when they mingle in this honey syrup.
You'll want to savor the syrup as much as you'll want to eat the plump fruit,
so serve this refreshing first course in goblets or footed dessert dishes.

1 cup sugar

½ cup water

3 tablespoons honey

3 sprigs fresh rosemary

6 large grapefruit

½ cup maraschino cherries with stems

Garnish: fresh rosemary sprigs

COMBINE first 4 ingredients in a saucepan. Bring to a boil over medium heat. Boil 5 minutes. Remove from heat, and let cool completely. Remove and discard rosemary.

PEEL and section grapefruit over a serving bowl to catch juice. Add grapefruit to bowl. Pour rosemary syrup over fruit sections. Add cherries. Cover and chill until ready to serve. Garnish, if desired. **Yield:** 10 servings.

SOUTHERN BRUNCH CASSEROLE

This is a hearty dish—bubbling full of bacon, eggs, and sharp Cheddar.

2 large baking potatoes, unpeeled and cubed

¼ cup butter or margarine

¼ cup all-purpose flour

1 cup milk

1 cup half-and-half

4 cups (16 ounces) shredded sharp Cheddar cheese

1 teaspoon dried Italian seasoning

½ teaspoon pepper

12 hard-cooked eggs, sliced

1 pound bacon, cooked and coarsely crumbled

2 cups soft whole wheat breadcrumbs (4 slices bread)

3 tablespoons butter or margarine, melted

Garnish: fresh herb sprigs

PLACE potato cubes in a large saucepan; cover with water. Boil 15 minutes or until just tender. Drain and cool.

MELT ¼ cup butter in a heavy saucepan over medium-low heat; add flour, stirring until smooth. Cook, stirring constantly, 1 minute. Gradually add milk and half-and-half; cook over medium heat, stirring constantly, until thickened and bubbly. Add cheese, Italian seasoning, and pepper, stirring constantly until cheese melts. Remove from heat.

LAYER half each of egg slices, bacon, and cheese sauce in a lightly greased 13- x 9- x 2-inch baking dish. Top with potato. Top with remaining egg slices, bacon, and cheese sauce.

COMBINE breadcrumbs and 3 tablespoons melted butter; sprinkle over casserole. Cover and chill overnight, if desired.

REMOVE casserole from refrigerator. Let stand at room temperature 30 minutes. Bake, uncovered, at 350° for 30 minutes or until thoroughly heated. Garnish, if desired. **Yield:** 10 servings.

BEATEN BISCUITS

Trade in your rolling pin for a food processor, and forget hours of endless rolling for the perfect beaten biscuit. These characteristically compact biscuits with flaky layers split easily to form perfect pockets for their traditional partner, country ham.

2 cups all-purpose flour
1 teaspoon salt
½ cup cold butter, cut into
     small pieces

⅓ cup ice water
   Country ham

POSITION knife blade in food processor bowl; add flour and salt. Process 5 seconds; add butter, and process 10 seconds or until mixture is crumbly.

POUR water through food chute with processor running; process until mixture forms a ball. Turn dough out onto a lightly floured surface. Roll dough into a ⅛-inch-thick rectangle. Fold dough in half lengthwise; cut with a 1-inch biscuit cutter. Place on an ungreased baking sheet. Prick top of each biscuit with a fork three times. Bake at 400° for 20 minutes or until lightly browned. Serve with country ham. **Yield:** 20 biscuits.

RUM-GLAZED COFFEE ROLLS

Canned biscuits give you a jump start on these sweet rolls that taste homemade.
Don't worry about how you arrange these sugar-coated biscuits in the pan—
during baking they expand into a coffee cake that separates easily into single rolls.

½ cup coarsely chopped pecans

1 cup firmly packed brown sugar

⅓ cup brewed coffee

¼ cup butter or margarine, melted

2 tablespoons dark rum

⅔ cup sugar

2 tablespoons instant coffee granules

2 (11-ounce) cans refrigerated buttermilk biscuits

⅓ cup butter or margarine, melted

SPRINKLE pecans in a heavily greased 12-cup Bundt pan. Combine brown sugar and next 3 ingredients, stirring well. Pour mixture into pan.

COMBINE ⅔ cup sugar and coffee granules in a shallow bowl; stir well. Separate biscuits; dip biscuits in ⅓ cup melted butter, and dredge in sugar mixture. Stand biscuits on edge around pan, placing 12 on outer side and 8 on inner side of pan.

BAKE at 350° for 28 minutes. Cool in pan on a wire rack 5 minutes. Invert onto a serving platter, and serve immediately. **Yield:** 20 rolls.

CINNAMON-SOUR CREAM STREUSEL LOAF

Sour cream makes this little loaf moist and luscious.

½ cup butter or margarine, softened

1 cup sugar

1 large egg

1¼ cups all-purpose flour

½ teaspoon baking powder

¼ teaspoon salt

½ cup sour cream

½ teaspoon vanilla extract

½ cup chopped pecans

¼ cup firmly packed brown sugar

1 tablespoon sugar

½ teaspoon ground cinnamon

BEAT butter at medium speed with an electric mixer until creamy; gradually add 1 cup sugar, beating well. Add egg, beating until blended.

COMBINE flour, baking powder, and salt; add to butter mixture alternately with sour cream, beginning and ending with flour mixture.

BEAT at low speed just until blended. Stir in vanilla.

COMBINE pecans and remaining 3 ingredients. Pour half of batter into a greased and floured 8½- x 4½- x 3-inch loafpan; sprinkle with half of pecan mixture. Pour remaining batter into pan; top with remaining pecan mixture.

BAKE at 350° for 1 hour or until wooden pick inserted in center comes out clean. (Cover with aluminum foil during last 15 minutes of baking to prevent excessive browning, if necessary.) Cool in pan on a wire rack 10 minutes; remove from pan, and cool completely. **Yield:** 1 loaf.

OVERNIGHT BLOODY MARYS

1 (46-ounce) can tomato juice	1 teaspoon salt
1 (46-ounce) can vegetable juice	½ teaspoon seasoned salt
1 cup lemon juice	3 cups vodka
½ cup water	Garnish: celery stalks or lime slices
2 tablespoons Worcestershire sauce	

COMBINE first 7 ingredients in a large container; stir well. Cover and chill at least 8 hours. Stir in vodka just before serving. Serve over ice. Garnish, if desired. **Yield:** 1 gallon.

MULLED WINE PUNCH

2 quarts Biltmore Estate Cardinal's Crest or other dry red wine	3 (3-inch) sticks cinnamon
	1½ teaspoons whole cloves
	1 teaspoon whole allspice
2 quarts apple juice	

COMBINE wine and apple juice in a large container. Tie spices in cheesecloth; add to wine mixture. Cover and chill wine mixture several hours or overnight.

POUR mixture into a large Dutch oven; bring to a boil. Reduce heat and simmer 3 to 5 minutes. Remove spice bag. Serve hot. **Yield:** 1 gallon.

Bloody Mary Lives On

The Bloody Mary was originally introduced to promote the sale of Smirnoff Vodka. This spicy concoction, presumably named after Mary I of England and her bloody reign, combines vodka, tomato juice, lemon juice, and Worcestershire sauce with its signature garnish of celery stalks or lime slices. It boosted the popularity of vodka worldwide, and by the 1970s, Americans were buying more vodka than whiskey. The martini and the screwdriver also owe their origins to the promotion of vodka.

Recipes for
EVERY DAY

MEALTIME MATTERS

ith a little creative attention, any meal can be memorable. Some things to consider:

• When planning a meal, **choose a focus** such as a theme or the entrée, and center your meal around it. As a rule, let variety be your guide. You'll find that foods prepared using different cooking methods will probably provide a nutritious and appealing meal.

• **Think about the color, flavor, texture, and size** of items on the plate. For example, try not to serve several round foods like meatballs, new potatoes, and brussels sprouts. Avoid too many mixtures like casseroles. And include contrasting colors instead of a monochromatic meal. Garnishes, such as herb sprigs, can add a splash of color, enlivening the plate.

• **Don't repeat flavors.** If you're serving a tomato appetizer, avoid serving tomatoes as a side dish. Introduce milder flavors before strong ones—too many hot and spicy foods could be overwhelming. Generally, it's a good idea to plan only one highly seasoned recipe and one starchy item in a menu.

• **Serve some foods hot, some cold.** Cold soups, chilled fruit, and vegetable salads provide welcome contrasts to hot entrées and side dishes. Tip: Chill the serving plates for cold foods, and warm the serving bowls with hot water to help keep foods like pastas, side dishes, and many entrées hot.

See our "Menus for All Seasons" beginning on page 12 for dozens of ideas to get you started.

Place-Setting Guide

hen setting the table, follow this guide. Add color and warmth with a placemat, or rest a charger (service plate) right on the table. The charger and flatware are placed 1" from the table's edge. Place the knife with its blade turned toward the plate; the dessert fork or spoon can be brought in with the dessert or placed European style (above the dinner plate). Place beverage glasses on the right and the bread and salad plates on the left. Add or eliminate pieces as needed.

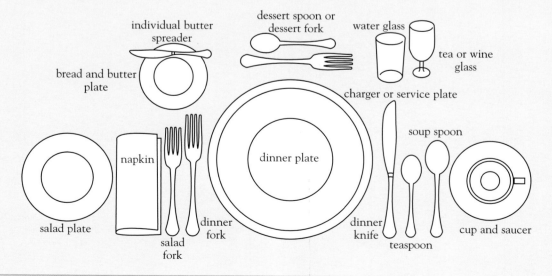

APPETIZERS & BEVERAGES

Sautéed Shrimp with
Cranberry-Citrus Salsa, page 83

ROASTED ONION DIP

This dip thickens as it chills and can double as a dressing for salad greens.

1 cup balsamic vinegar
1 large purple onion, cut in half crosswise (about 1 pound)
1 teaspoon beef bouillon granules
½ (0.4-ounce) package Ranch-style salad dressing mix (¾ teaspoon)

¼ teaspoon garlic powder
¼ to ½ teaspoon pepper
2 (3-ounce) packages cream cheese
1 (8-ounce) carton sour cream
¾ cup mayonnaise

BRING vinegar to a boil in a 10-inch cast-iron skillet over medium-high heat. Remove from heat; place onion, cut side down, in skillet. Roast, uncovered, at 400° for 50 minutes or until onion is tender and brown. Let cool.

COMBINE onion, bouillon granules, and next 3 ingredients in an electric blender or food processor; cover and process until almost smooth, stopping once to scrape down sides.

ADD cream cheese to blender; cover and process 3 minutes, stopping once to scrape down sides. Add sour cream and mayonnaise. Cover and process 1 minute. Cover and chill 30 minutes. Serve with assorted fresh vegetables and crackers. **Yield:** 4 cups.

Winemaker's Notes: *Serve with Biltmore Estate Zinfandel Blanc de Noir*

WHITE BEAN HUMMUS

1 (15-ounce) can cannellini or other white beans, rinsed and drained
¼ cup tahini
3 tablespoons lemon juice
1½ teaspoons ground cumin

¼ teaspoon salt
¼ teaspoon ground red pepper
2 cloves garlic
2 tablespoons minced fresh parsley

PROCESS first 7 ingredients in a food processor until mixture is smooth; stir in parsley. Serve with pita chips or toasted baguette slices. **Yield:** 1¼ cups.

GRILLED CORN SALSA

3 ears fresh shucked corn

1 large sweet onion, cut into
½-inch-thick slices

1 red bell pepper, halved

2 large tomatoes, seeded and
chopped

2 jalapeño peppers, seeded and
minced

2 cloves garlic, minced

¼ cup chopped fresh cilantro

½ teaspoon salt

¼ teaspoon ground cumin

1 tablespoon olive oil

1 tablespoon lime juice

Garnish: fresh cilantro sprig

GRILL first 3 ingredients, covered with grill lid, over medium-hot coals (350° to 400°) 8 to 10 minutes or until tender, turning occasionally. Cut corn kernels from cobs. Coarsely chop onion and red bell pepper halves.

COMBINE grilled vegetables, tomato, and next 7 ingredients in a large bowl; cover and chill 2 hours or up to 2 days. Serve with tortilla chips or grilled chicken, fish, or beef. Garnish, if desired. **Yield:** 5 cups.

Winemaker's Notes: Serve with Biltmore Estate Cabernet Blanc de Noir

SMOKED SALMON PÂTÉ

6 ounces smoked salmon

1 (3-ounce) package cream
cheese, softened

2 tablespoons butter or
margarine, softened

½ teaspoon hot sauce

1 teaspoon lemon juice

2 tablespoons coarsely chopped
purple onion

Garnishes: chopped purple
onion, green onion tops

PULSE first 6 ingredients in a food processor until salmon is coarsely chopped, stopping once to scrape down sides. Serve immediately, or cover and chill 2 hours. Garnish, if desired. Serve with celery sticks or assorted crackers. **Yield:** 1 cup.

Winemaker's Notes: Serve with Château Biltmore Chardonnay

KAHLÚA-PECAN BRIE

1 (15-ounce) round Brie
½ cup chopped pecans, toasted
2 tablespoons brown sugar
2½ tablespoons Kahlúa or other coffee-flavored liqueur

REMOVE rind from top of cheese, cutting to within ½ inch of edge. Place on an oven-safe dish.

COMBINE pecans, brown sugar, and Kahlúa; spread over cheese. Bake at 350° for 5 minutes or just until soft. Serve immediately with gingersnaps or apple slices. **Yield:** 8 appetizer servings.

SPINACH-HERB CHEESECAKE

Make this savory cheesecake the star of your next wine and cheese gathering. The stately presentation pleases the eye, while the savory flavor delights the palate.

2 large tomatoes, sliced
¾ teaspoon salt, divided
¾ teaspoon pepper, divided
¼ cup pine nuts, toasted
¼ cup Italian-seasoned breadcrumbs
2 tablespoons butter or margarine, melted
3 (8-ounce) packages cream cheese, softened
1 (15-ounce) carton ricotta cheese
1 (8-ounce) package feta cheese, crumbled
3 large eggs
4 cups loosely packed shredded fresh spinach
2 cloves garlic, pressed
2 tablespoons all-purpose flour
1 tablespoon chopped fresh dill

SPRINKLE tomato slices with ¼ teaspoon salt and ¼ teaspoon pepper. Drain on paper towels 10 minutes.

PROCESS pine nuts in a food processor until ground. Stir together pine nuts, breadcrumbs, and melted butter. Press into bottom of a 9-inch spring-form pan. Bake at 350° for 10 minutes. Cool in pan on a wire rack.

BEAT cream cheese at medium speed with an electric mixer until creamy; add ricotta cheese, feta cheese, and eggs, beating until blended. Stir in spinach, next 3 ingredients, remaining ½ teaspoon salt, and remaining ½ teaspoon pepper. Pour into prepared crust.

BAKE at 325° for 15 minutes. Top with tomato slices, and bake 30 more minutes or until set. Turn oven off; leave cheesecake in oven 20 minutes. Cool on a wire rack 10 minutes. Gently run a knife around edge of cheesecake, and carefully remove sides of pan; cool 10 more minutes. Serve warm or cold. **Yield:** 12 appetizer or 8 main-dish servings.

Winemaker's Notes: Serve with Biltmore Estate Cardinal's Crest

Bistro: Chef's Choice
BRUSCHETTA
These little appetizers are delightful with or without the Gorgonzola cheese.

2 medium-size red bell peppers	1½ teaspoons chopped fresh parsley
2 medium-size green bell peppers	½ teaspoon salt
2 Roma tomatoes, seeded and diced (about ½ cup)	½ teaspoon freshly ground black pepper
¼ cup finely chopped purple onion	1 French baguette, cut into ½-inch slices
2 tablespoons balsamic vinegar	½ cup crumbled Gorgonzola cheese (optional)
2 tablespoons olive oil	
1½ teaspoons chopped fresh basil	

CUT bell peppers in half crosswise; discard seeds. Place peppers, skin side up, on a baking sheet; flatten with palm of hand. Broil peppers 5½ inches from heat 5 to 10 minutes or until charred. Place peppers in a heavy-duty, zip-top plastic bag; seal and let stand 10 minutes to loosen skins.

PEEL peppers, and discard skins. Dice peppers; combine diced pepper, tomato, and next 7 ingredients; toss gently. Cover and chill.

PLACE bread slices on ungreased baking sheets. Bake at 400° for 6 minutes or until lightly toasted, turning once. Using a slotted spoon, spoon about 1 tablespoon pepper mixture onto each bread slice. Serve immediately or, if desired, top each slice with about 1 teaspoon Gorgonzola cheese and broil 3 inches from heat for 2 minutes. Serve immediately. **Yield:** 26 appetizers.

Winemaker's Notes: Serve with Biltmore Estate Zinfandel Blanc de Noir

Gouda-Cashew Bouchées

Bouchée is French for "small patty" or "mouthful." Each one of these savory "mouthfuls" is crowned with a buttery cashew.

1½	cups (6 ounces) shredded Gouda cheese	1½	cups all-purpose flour
½	cup butter or margarine, softened	1	teaspoon dry mustard
		⅛	teaspoon salt
		24	whole cashews

COMBINE cheese and butter in a large mixing bowl; beat at medium speed with an electric mixer until blended.

COMBINE flour, mustard, and salt; add to cheese mixture, beating until dough is no longer crumbly. Shape into 24 (1-inch) balls. Place on lightly greased baking sheets; press a cashew on top of each ball. Bake at 375° for 16 to 18 minutes or until lightly browned. Let cool on wire racks. **Yield:** 2 dozen.

Winemaker's Notes: Serve with Biltmore Estate Blanc de Blanc-Brut

Stuffed Shiitakes Parmigiana

12	large shiitake mushrooms	12	round buttery crackers, crushed
2	tablespoons butter or margarine	3	tablespoons freshly grated Parmesan cheese
1	medium onion, diced	1	tablespoon chopped fresh parsley
½	(4-ounce) package sliced pepperoni, chopped	½	teaspoon seasoned salt
¼	cup diced green bell pepper	¼	teaspoon dried oregano
1	clove garlic, minced		Dash of black pepper
⅓	cup chicken broth		

REMOVE and discard stems from mushrooms. Place mushroom caps in a 15- x 10- x 2-inch jellyroll pan; set aside.

MELT butter in a large skillet over medium-high heat. Add onion and next 3 ingredients; sauté until tender. Add broth and remaining 6 ingredients. Spoon mixture into mushroom caps. Add water to pan to depth of ⅛ inch. Bake at 325° for 25 minutes; transfer mushrooms to serving plate, and serve immediately. **Yield:** 1 dozen.

Sautéed Shrimp with Cranberry-Citrus Salsa

Serve this impressive dish with our crisp Sauvignon Blanc as a seated prelude to a special meal. See the shrimp on page 77.

4 pounds unpeeled large fresh shrimp
½ cup orange juice
¼ cup minced garlic, divided
1 tablespoon olive oil
½ teaspoon salt
¼ teaspoon freshly ground pepper
Cranberry-Citrus Salsa
Garnish: fresh Italian parsley sprigs

PEEL shrimp, leaving tails intact; devein, if desired.

COMBINE orange juice and 2 tablespoons garlic in a shallow dish or large heavy-duty, zip-top plastic bag; add shrimp. Cover or seal; chill 2 hours, turning occasionally. Drain.

SAUTÉ remaining 2 tablespoons garlic in 1 tablespoon hot oil in a large skillet until tender.

ADD shrimp, and sauté 3 to 5 minutes or just until shrimp turn pink. Remove from heat. Sprinkle shrimp with salt and pepper, and toss. Serve with Cranberry-Citrus Salsa. Garnish, if desired. **Yield:** 10 to 12 servings.

CRANBERRY-CITRUS SALSA

1 pink grapefruit, peeled, sectioned, and chopped
2 teaspoons grated orange rind
1 orange, peeled, sectioned, and chopped
1 cup fresh cranberries, halved
½ green bell pepper, diced
¼ cup chopped purple onion
1 clove garlic, pressed
2 tablespoons minced fresh Italian parsley
2 tablespoons fresh orange juice
¼ teaspoon salt

STIR together all ingredients; cover and chill. **Yield:** 2 cups.

Winemaker's Notes: Serve with Biltmore Estate Sauvignon Blanc

The Art of Picnicking

Whether you're celebrating with friends or sharing a romantic dinner, let both the location and occasion determine how you'll serve your picnic fare. Start by using our meal planning hints on page 76 to help you plan a menu to suit your theme.

Adorable picnic baskets look great, but they aren't suitable for keeping food at the right temperature if your meal takes you far from home. Remember the two-hour rule: Meats, poultry, seafood, eggs, and milk (and foods that contain these ingredients) should not be left at room temperature—or outside in the heat—for more than two hours.

Insulated coolers are your best bet to transport food. The key: keep cold foods COLD and hot foods HOT. A cold source such as ice, commercial ice packs, or a frozen jug of water should be included to maintain cold temperatures. Take advantage of casserole quilts, baking dish baskets, or cardboard boxes lined with several thicknesses of newspaper to help hold in the heat of warmer items.

(Continued on next page)

Bistro: Chef's Choice

CREAM OF PORTOBELLO MUSHROOM SOUP

Don't skimp on the heavy whipping cream for this rich and creamy soup. 'Heavy whipping cream' has at least 36% milk fat making it thicker and a better choice for cream soups and desserts. Light whipping cream, commonly labeled 'whipping cream' in the grocery store, contains about 30% milk fat.

3 tablespoons olive oil	1 cup half-and-half
1 small onion, chopped (about 1⅓ cups)	1 cup heavy whipping cream
1 pound portobello mushrooms, chopped	½ teaspoon ground white pepper
6 cups chicken broth	Garnish: heavy whipping cream

HEAT olive oil in a heavy 4½-quart Dutch oven over medium heat. Add onion; cook 5 minutes, stirring occasionally or until slightly tender. Add mushrooms; cook 4 minutes, stirring often. Pour in chicken broth; simmer, uncovered, 35 minutes.

PROCESS half of mushroom mixture in an electric blender until smooth. Repeat procedure with remaining mushroom mixture. Return mushroom mixture to pan. Pour in half-and-half and heavy cream; bring to a simmer. Simmer, uncovered, 10 minutes. Stir in pepper. To serve, drizzle about 1 teaspoon heavy cream over surface of soup in individual bowls, if desired, and serve immediately. **Yield:** 8½ cups.

Winemaker's Notes: *Serve with Château Biltmore Chardonnay*

CHILLED SUMMER BERRIES AND SPARKLING WINE SOUP

This fruit soup is a classic addition to your summer picnic menu.

1 cup fresh raspberries	½ cup fresh lime juice (about 2 limes)
1 cup sliced fresh strawberries	¼ cup sugar
1 cup fresh blackberries	2 cups Biltmore Estate Blanc de Blanc-Brut Sparkling Wine or other sparkling white wine
1 medium banana, peeled and diced	
1 medium peach, diced (about 1 cup)	
1 cup fresh orange juice (about 3 oranges)	

COMBINE fruit, juices, and sugar; stir gently. Let stand 15 minutes. Process fruit mixture in container of an electric blender until smooth. Pour fruit mixture through a cheesecloth-lined wire-mesh strainer into a large bowl, discarding seeds. Stir in sparkling wine. Chill. **Yield:** 6 cups.

Bistro: Chef's Choice

STRAWBERRY-WINE COOLER

2 cups fresh strawberries (about 1 pint), trimmed	1 (750-milliliter) bottle Biltmore Estate Sauvignon Blanc or other dry white wine, chilled
⅓ cup sugar	

COMBINE strawberries and sugar in a small bowl; let stand 10 minutes. Combine strawberry mixture and wine in container of an electric blender; process until smooth, stopping once to scrape down sides. Pour mixture through a cheesecloth-lined wire-mesh strainer into a pitcher, discarding seeds. Chill; serve over ice. **Yield:** 4 cups.

(Continued from previous page)

A romantic picnic for two may demand packing crystal and fine china: wrap breakables in cloth napkins and your tablecloth to serve double duty. A casual tailgate with friends could enlist the simplest of serving ware—paper and plastic. If you haven't browsed the aisles of disposable dinnerware in the market lately, you're in for a pleasant surprise.

Before you leave for the picnic, think about every element needed for the meal. Include items like serving utensils, a corkscrew, sharp knife, a can opener, and cutting board. Think about cleanup, too. Take trash bags, bottled water, and paper towels for handy use.

The finishing touch—the centerpiece—can be simple yet beautiful. Take a wide-mouthed jar, fill it with water, and use flowers either from your yard or the picnic site (picked with permission, of course).

Blueberry Lemonade

BLUEBERRY LEMONADE

Plump fresh blueberries color this lemonade a pretty purplish pink.

⅓ cup fresh lemon juice (about
    4 small lemons)
2 cups water
2 cups fresh or frozen
    blueberries, thawed

½ cup sugar
   Garnish: lemon slices

PROCESS first 4 ingredients in an electric blender until smooth, stopping once to scrape down sides. Pour through a wire-mesh strainer into a pitcher, discarding fruit solids. Serve over ice, and garnish, if desired. **Yield:** 4½ cups.

FRUIT AND MINT ICED TEA

Dozens of mint varieties are available for growing and cooking. Try spearmint or apple mint in this tea. If your grocery doesn't have a wide herb selection, find fresh herbs at most garden centers.

1 quart boiling water
8 regular-size tea bags
½ cup fresh mint leaves,
    crushed
1½ cups sugar
1 (6-ounce) can frozen
    lemonade concentrate,
    thawed and undiluted

1 (6-ounce) can frozen
    limeade concentrate,
    thawed and undiluted
¾ cup orange juice
3 quarts cold water

POUR 1 quart boiling water over tea bags and mint; cover and steep 30 minutes. Remove and discard tea bags. Stir in sugar and remaining ingredients.

POUR tea through a wire-mesh strainer into a large pitcher, discarding mint. Chill. Serve over ice. **Yield:** about 4½ quarts.

POINSETTIA PUNCH

2 (10-ounce) packages frozen
  raspberries, thawed
1 (6-ounce) can frozen pink
  lemonade concentrate,
  thawed and undiluted
¼ cup sugar

1 (750-milliliter) bottle
  Biltmore Estate Zinfandel
  Blanc de Noir or other rosé
1 (2-liter) bottle raspberry
  ginger ale or ginger ale,
  chilled

COMBINE first 3 ingredients in container of an electric blender; process until smooth. Pour mixture through a wire-mesh strainer into a large container, discarding seeds.

COMBINE raspberry mixture and wine; cover and chill. Stir in ginger ale, and serve immediately. **Yield:** about 6 quarts.

HOT WHITE CHOCOLATE BRANDY ALEXANDER

3½ cups milk
½ teaspoon vanilla extract
⅛ teaspoon salt
6 ounces white chocolate,
  finely chopped

⅓ cup brandy
3 tablespoons white crème
  de cacao
Garnishes: whipped cream,
  white chocolate shavings

COMBINE first 3 ingredients in a medium saucepan; cook over medium heat until thoroughly heated (do not boil). Remove from heat; gradually stir about one-fourth of hot mixture into chocolate in a small bowl, stirring with a wire whisk until chocolate melts. Add to remaining hot mixture, stirring constantly.

STIR in brandy and crème de cacao. Pour into glasses. Garnish, if desired. Serve immediately. **Yield:** 4½ cups.

BREADS

Refrigerator Yeast Rolls, page 96

RASPBERRY CRUMBLE COFFEE CAKE

If you prefer one large coffee cake instead of 2 round ones, use a greased
13- x 9- x 2-inch pan, and bake as directed below.

⅔ cup sugar

¼ cup cornstarch

¾ cup cold water

2 cups fresh or frozen
    raspberries

1 tablespoon lemon juice

3 cups all-purpose flour

1 tablespoon baking powder

1 cup sugar

1 teaspoon salt

1 teaspoon ground cinnamon

¼ teaspoon ground mace

1 cup butter or margarine

2 large eggs, lightly beaten

1 cup milk

1 teaspoon vanilla extract

½ cup all-purpose flour

½ cup sugar

¼ cup butter or margarine

¼ cup sliced almonds

COMBINE ⅔ cup sugar, cornstarch, and water in a medium saucepan, stirring until smooth; add raspberries. Cook over medium heat, stirring constantly, until mixture thickens and comes to a boil. Boil 1 minute, stirring constantly. Remove from heat, and stir in lemon juice; let cool.

COMBINE 3 cups flour and next 5 ingredients; cut in 1 cup butter with a pastry blender or 2 knives until mixture is crumbly. Add eggs, milk, and vanilla; stir well.

SPOON one-fourth of batter into each of two greased 8-inch round cakepans. Spread raspberry mixture over batter in pans, dividing evenly. Top evenly with remaining batter.

COMBINE ½ cup flour and ½ cup sugar in a small bowl; stir well. Cut in ¼ cup butter with pastry blender or 2 knives until mixture is crumbly. Stir in sliced almonds. Sprinkle almond mixture evenly over batter in pans. Bake at 350° for 40 to 45 minutes or until a wooden pick inserted in center of cakes comes out clean. Cool in pans on wire racks 10 minutes; remove cakes from pans, if desired, and let cool completely on wire racks. **Yield:** two 8-inch coffee cakes.

CHOCOLATE CHIP BANANA-NUT BREAD

2 cups all-purpose flour	2 large eggs, lightly beaten
1 teaspoon baking soda	½ cup vegetable oil
1 teaspoon salt	½ cup chopped walnuts
¾ cup sugar	½ cup semisweet chocolate
1⅓ cups mashed ripe banana	morsels
(about 3 medium)	

COMBINE first 4 ingredients in a large bowl; make a well in center of mixture. Combine mashed banana, eggs, and oil; add banana mixture to dry ingredients, stirring just until moistened. Stir in walnuts and chocolate morsels.

POUR batter into a greased 8½- x 4½- x 3-inch loafpan. Bake at 350° for 1 hour or until a wooden pick inserted in center comes out clean. Cool in pan on a wire rack 10 minutes; remove from pan, and cool on rack. **Yield:** 1 loaf.

BUTTERNUT SPICE LOAF

1 (2-pound) butternut squash	1 teaspoon ground cinnamon
½ cup butter, softened	½ teaspoon ground nutmeg
1½ cups sugar	½ teaspoon ground allspice
2 large eggs	¼ teaspoon ground ginger
2 cups self-rising flour	½ cup chopped pecans

CUT squash in half lengthwise; remove seeds. Place cut side down in a shallow pan; add water to a depth of ½ inch. Cover with foil, and bake at 400° for 1 hour or until tender; drain. Scoop out pulp; mash. Discard shell. Measure 1¾ cups pulp; reserve any remaining pulp for other uses.

BEAT butter at medium speed with an electric mixer until creamy; gradually add sugar, beating well. Add eggs, one at a time, beating after each addition.

COMBINE flour and spices; add to butter mixture alternately with squash pulp, beginning and ending with flour mixture. Stir in pecans. Spoon batter into a greased and floured 9- x 5- x 3-inch loafpan; bake at 350° for 1 hour to 1 hour and 10 minutes or until a wooden pick inserted in center comes out clean. Cool in pan on a wire rack 10 minutes. Remove from pan, and let cool completely on wire rack. **Yield:** 1 loaf.

Lemon Tea Bread

LEMON TEA BREAD

A small crack down the top center of this bread is characteristic of quick loaves.
So don't panic—it's usually there.

¾ cup milk

1 tablespoon chopped fresh
    lemon balm or 1 table-
    spoon fresh lemon juice

1 tablespoon chopped fresh
    lemon thyme or 1 teaspoon
    dried thyme

½ cup butter or margarine,
    softened

1 cup sugar

2 large eggs

2 cups all-purpose flour

1½ teaspoons baking powder

¼ teaspoon salt

1 tablespoon grated lemon rind
    Lemon Glaze

COMBINE first 3 ingredients in a small saucepan, and bring to a boil.
Remove mixture from heat; cover and let stand 5 minutes. Cool.

BEAT butter at medium speed with an electric mixer until creamy, and
gradually add sugar, beating mixture well. Add eggs, one at a time, beating
after each addition.

COMBINE flour, baking powder, and salt; add to butter mixture alternately with milk mixture, beginning and ending with flour mixture. Mix
after each addition. Stir in lemon rind.

POUR into a greased and floured 9- x 5- x 3-inch loafpan. Bake at 325°
for 50 minutes or until a wooden pick inserted in center comes out clean.
Cool in pan on a wire rack 10 minutes. Remove from pan, and let cool
completely on wire rack. Pour Lemon Glaze over bread. **Yield:** 1 loaf.

LEMON GLAZE

1 cup sifted powdered sugar

2 tablespoons fresh lemon juice

COMBINE powdered sugar and lemon juice in a small bowl; stir until
smooth. **Yield:** ⅓ cup.

PUMPKIN-MOLASSES MUFFINS

Molasses lends old-fashioned flavor to these moist, rich muffins.

½	cup butter or margarine, softened	¼	cup molasses
¾	cup firmly packed brown sugar	1¾	cups all-purpose flour
		1	tablespoon baking soda
1	large egg	¼	teaspoon salt
1	cup canned pumpkin	¾	teaspoon ground ginger
		¼	cup chopped pecans

BEAT butter at medium speed with an electric mixer until creamy; gradually add brown sugar, beating well. Add egg, beating well. Add pumpkin and molasses, beating well.

COMBINE flour and next 3 ingredients; gradually add to pumpkin mixture, beating at medium-low just until blended. Stir in pecans. Spoon into greased muffin pans, filling three-fourths full. Bake at 375° for 20 minutes. Remove from pans immediately. **Yield:** 1 dozen.

HERB BISCUITS

4	cups all-purpose flour	1	tablespoon chopped fresh basil
1	tablespoon plus 2 teaspoons baking powder		
		2	teaspoons chopped fresh thyme
½	teaspoon baking soda		
¾	teaspoon salt	½	cup butter
1	teaspoon pepper	1	cup milk
2	tablespoons chopped fresh dill	1	(8-ounce) carton sour cream

COMBINE first 8 ingredients in a large bowl. Cut in butter with a pastry blender or 2 knives until mixture is crumbly.

COMBINE milk and sour cream; add to flour mixture, stirring just until dry ingredients are moistened.

TURN dough out onto a floured surface; knead 4 or 5 times. Roll dough to ½-inch thickness; cut into rounds with a 2-inch biscuit cutter. Place on a lightly greased baking sheet. Bake at 450° for 11 minutes or until golden. **Yield:** about 2½ dozen.

CINNAMON SCONES

3 cups all-purpose flour	2 large eggs, lightly beaten
½ cup sugar	¾ cup milk
1 tablespoon baking powder	1 large egg
½ teaspoon salt	1 tablespoon water
½ teaspoon ground cinnamon	1 tablespoon cinnamon-sugar
¼ cup plus 1 tablespoon butter	

COMBINE first 5 ingredients in a large bowl; cut in butter with a pastry blender or 2 knives until mixture is crumbly. Combine beaten eggs and milk; add to dry ingredients, stirring just until moistened.

TURN dough out onto a lightly floured surface; knead lightly 4 or 5 times. Shape into a ball. Pat ball into a 9½-inch circle on a lightly greased baking sheet; cut into 8 wedges, using a sharp knife. (Do not separate wedges.)

COMBINE 1 egg and water; beat with a wire whisk until blended. Brush dough with egg mixture. Sprinkle with 1 tablespoon cinnamon-sugar. Bake at 425° for 10 to 12 minutes or until lightly browned. Serve warm. **Yield:** 8 scones.

SAGE CORNBREAD

This moist, dense cornbread with herb appeal forms a tasty base for a hearty dressing.

1 cup all-purpose flour	2 large eggs
¾ cup cornmeal	1 cup buttermilk
1½ teaspoons baking powder	3 tablespoons butter or
½ teaspoon baking soda	margarine, melted
2 tablespoons chopped fresh sage	2 tablespoons honey

COMBINE first 5 ingredients in a large bowl; make a well in center of mixture. Combine eggs and next 3 ingredients; beat with a wire whisk until blended. Add to dry ingredients, stirring just until blended.

POUR into a greased 9-inch square pan. Bake at 425° for 20 to 25 minutes or until golden. Cut into squares, and serve warm with honey. **Yield:** 8 servings.

Winemaker's Notes: Any wine pairs nicely. Try Biltmore Estate Special Reserve Chenin Blanc.

PARMESAN POPOVERS

1 cup bread flour	1 tablespoon chopped fresh
1 cup milk	basil
1 large egg	$\frac{1}{4}$ teaspoon salt
2 egg whites	2 tablespoons grated Parmesan
2 teaspoons vegetable oil	cheese
2 teaspoons sugar	

COMBINE first 8 ingredients; beat at low speed with an electric mixer just until blended and smooth. Stir in Parmesan cheese. Fill six 6-ounce lightly greased custard cups three-fourths full. Bake at 425° for 25 to 30 minutes or until crusty and dark brown. Serve popovers immediately. **Yield:** 6 popovers.

REFRIGERATOR YEAST ROLLS

The dough for these rolls (pictured on page 89) can remain
in the refrigerator up to 5 days.

1 package active dry yeast	1$\frac{3}{4}$ cups milk
$\frac{1}{4}$ cup warm water (105° to 115°)	$\frac{1}{4}$ cup vegetable oil
	1$\frac{1}{2}$ teaspoons salt
$\frac{1}{4}$ cup plus 2 tablespoons sugar, divided	6 cups bread flour
	Melted butter

COMBINE yeast, water, and 1 teaspoon sugar; let stand 5 minutes. Combine remaining sugar, milk, oil, and salt in a saucepan; cook over medium heat until sugar dissolves, stirring occasionally. Cool to 115°. Add yeast mixture; stir well. Place flour in a large bowl. Gradually add liquid mixture to flour, stirring to make a stiff dough. Place in a well-greased bowl, turning to coat top. Let stand at room temperature 10 minutes. Cover and chill at least 8 hours.

TO MAKE rolls, punch dough down; turn out onto floured surface, and knead 2 or 3 times. Divide dough into thirds. Working with 1 portion at a time, shape dough into 12 balls. Place balls in a lightly greased 9-inch round cakepan. Repeat procedure with remaining portions of dough.

COVER and let rise in a warm place (85°), free from drafts, 45 minutes or until doubled in bulk. Bake at 400° for 10 to 12 minutes or until golden. Brush tops of rolls with melted butter. **Yield:** 3 dozen.

FETA CHEESE BREAD

Chunks of creamy white feta cheese add rich flavor to this delicious bread.
Use rapid-rise yeast, which needs only one rising—that's half
the rising time of active dry yeast.

1½ cups milk	1 package rapid-rise yeast
¼ cup water	¼ cup butter or margarine, softened and divided
¼ cup shortening	
4 to 4½ cups all-purpose flour, divided	4 ounces feta cheese, crumbled and divided
2 teaspoons sugar	2 tablespoons butter or margarine, melted
½ teaspoon salt	

COMBINE first 3 ingredients in a saucepan; heat until shortening melts. Cool to 120° to 130°.

COMBINE 2 cups flour, sugar, salt, and yeast in a large mixing bowl. Add milk mixture, beating at low speed with an electric mixer. Beat 2 minutes at medium speed. Stir in enough remaining flour to make a soft dough. Turn dough out onto a floured surface; knead lightly 4 or 5 times. Divide dough in half.

ROLL 1 portion of dough into a 16- x 8-inch rectangle; spread with half of softened butter, and sprinkle with half of cheese. Roll up dough, starting at long side; pinch ends to seal. Place dough, seam side down, in a well-greased French bread pan.

REPEAT procedure with remaining dough, softened butter, and cheese. Brush each loaf with 1 tablespoon melted butter. Cover and let rise in a warm place (85°), free from drafts, 45 minutes or until doubled in bulk.

BAKE, uncovered, at 375° for 15 minutes. Reduce temperature to 350°, and bake 20 minutes or until loaves sound hollow when tapped. Remove from pans immediately; cool on wire racks. **Yield:** 2 loaves.

Winemaker's Notes: Biltmore Estate Cabernet Sauvignon

Bread Therapy

*T*here's a certain satisfaction that comes from baking home-made bread. For some, working the dough, both kneading and punching, is therapeutic. For your next "thera-py" session, here are some pointers:

• *Use the heel of one or both hands to knead yeast dough and develop its structure.*

• *After dough has risen, punch it down with your fist and fold dough into the center. Then it's ready to shape and bake.*

• *After baking, remove bread from the pan immediately, unless the recipe specifies otherwise, and place it on a wire rack. This is a good time to brush the hot loaf with melt-ed butter. Once the loaf is cool, use a bread knife (a long, slender knife with a serrated blade) and a gentle sawing motion to make a neat cut.*

CINNAMON PULL-AWAY BREAD

½ cup chopped pecans

½ cup sugar

1½ teaspoons ground cinnamon

1 (25-ounce) package frozen roll dough

3 tablespoons butter or margarine, melted

STIR together first 3 ingredients, and sprinkle one-third of mixture into a buttered 12-cup Bundt pan.

PLACE half of frozen rolls in bottom of pan, and drizzle with half of butter. Sprinkle with half of remaining pecan mixture. Repeat procedure with remaining frozen rolls, butter, and pecan mixture. Let rise in a warm place (85°), free from drafts, 2 hours or until dough is doubled in bulk.

BAKE at 350° for 30 minutes, shielding with aluminum foil after 20 minutes to prevent excessive browning. Loosen bread from sides of pan with a knife, and cool in pan 5 minutes; invert onto a serving plate. **Yield:** 1 loaf.

Bistro: Chef's Choice
FOCACCIA

2¼ cups very warm water (120° to 130°)

6½ cups bread flour

¼ cup olive oil

1 tablespoon salt

2 tablespoons dried basil

2 tablespoons dried thyme

1 tablespoon dried oregano

2 tablespoons rapid-rise yeast

¼ cup olive oil

POUR water into a heavy-duty mixer. Add flour and next 5 ingredients. Stir at low speed 45 seconds using a dough hook attachment. Add yeast to center of mixture; stir 45 seconds. Increase to second speed; mix 6 to 7 minutes.

COVER and let rise in a warm place (85°), free from drafts, 30 minutes or until doubled in bulk. Punch dough down; divide in half.

BRUSH two 15- x 10- x 1-inch jellyroll pans with 2 tablespoons olive oil each. Roll each dough portion into a 15- x 10-inch rectangle, and place in prepared pans. Cover and let rise in a warm place 20 minutes or until doubled.

USING fingertips, dimple the surface of the dough in both pans. Bake at 375° for 20 minutes or until golden. Cut or tear into squares. **Yield:** 16 servings.

ENTRÉES

Beef Filet with
Orange Cream, page 100

Rib Roast with Mustard Sauce

1 (3-pound) boneless rib roast	1 teaspoon coarsely ground
1 cup vegetable oil	pepper
²/₃ cup dry sherry	¹/₂ teaspoon onion salt
1 tablespoon chopped fresh	¹/₄ cup whipping cream, whipped
thyme	¹/₄ cup sour cream
1 tablespoon chopped fresh	2 tablespoons prepared mustard
rosemary	Dash of hot sauce

TRIM fat from roast. Place roast in a shallow dish. Combine oil and next 5 ingredients, stirring well. Pour mixture over roast. Cover and marinate in refrigerator 8 to 10 hours, turning occasionally.

REMOVE roast from marinade; bring marinade to a boil, and set aside. Place roast on a rack in a roasting pan. Insert meat thermometer into thickest part of roast, if desired. Bake at 350° for 1 hour and 45 minutes or until meat thermometer registers 150° (medium rare), basting roast frequently with marinade.

LET roast stand 15 minutes; cut diagonally across grain into thin slices. Transfer sliced meat to a serving platter, and keep warm.

COMBINE whipped cream, sour cream, mustard, and hot sauce in a bowl, stirring gently. Serve sauce with roast. **Yield:** 10 servings.

Winemaker's Notes: Serve with Biltmore Estate Cardinal's Crest

Beef Filets with Orange Cream
(pictured on page 99)

4 (6- to 8-ounce) beef	2 tablespoons orange
tenderloin steaks	marmalade
¹/₂ teaspoon cracked black	1 to 2 tablespoons prepared
pepper (optional)	horseradish
¹/₂ pint whipping cream	Garnish: orange rind curls

SPRINKLE steaks with cracked pepper, if desired.

GRILL steaks, covered with grill lid, over medium-hot coals (350° to 400°) 4 to 6 minutes on each side or to desired degree of doneness. Bring whipping cream, marmalade, and horseradish to a boil over medium-high heat, stirring constantly; reduce heat, and simmer 5 minutes or until thickened, stirring often. Serve immediately with steaks; garnish, if desired. **Yield:** 4 servings.

Winemaker's Notes: Serve with Biltmore Estate Chardonnay Sur Lies

GRILLED BEEF SALAD WITH HONEY-MUSTARD DRESSING

1 cup olive oil	$^1/_4$ teaspoon salt
$^1/_3$ cup balsamic vinegar	1 (2-pound) flank steak
$^1/_2$ teaspoon freshly ground pepper	12 cups mixed salad greens Honey-Mustard Dressing

PROCESS first 4 ingredients in an electric blender on low speed until smooth. Place flank steak in a large heavy-duty, zip-top plastic bag; pour marinade over steak. Seal bag, and marinate in refrigerator 3 hours, turning steak occasionally.

REMOVE steak from marinade, discarding marinade. Grill steak, covered with grill lid, over hot coals (400° to 500°) 7 to 8 minutes on each side or until a meat thermometer inserted in steak registers 150° (medium rare). Remove from heat; let steak cool at least 10 minutes. Cut steak diagonally into thin slices. Place over greens and drizzle with Honey-Mustard Dressing. **Yield:** 8 servings.

Bistro: Chef's Choice
HONEY-MUSTARD DRESSING

$^1/_2$ cup Dijon mustard	2 tablespoons egg substitute
2 tablespoons honey	$^1/_4$ cup champagne vinegar
$^1/_4$ teaspoon salt	2 cups olive oil
$^1/_4$ teaspoon freshly ground pepper	

PROCESS first 4 ingredients in an electric blender on low speed until smooth. Add egg substitute and vinegar; pulse until blended. With blender on low, gradually add oil in a steady stream; process until blended. **Yield:** $2^2/_3$ cups.

Winemaker's Notes: Serve with Biltmore Estate Chardonnay Sur Lies

BEEF BOURGUIGNON

1/2 cup olive oil	3 shallots, finely chopped
1 1/2 cups Biltmore Estate Cabernet Sauvignon or other dry red wine	3 cloves garlic, minced
	3/4 teaspoon salt, divided
	3/4 teaspoon pepper, divided
3 1/2 pounds boneless top sirloin roast, cut into 1-inch cubes*	1/4 cup all-purpose flour
	1 (14 1/2-ounce) can beef broth
	3 tablespoons butter or margarine
3 cups Biltmore Estate Cabernet Sauvignon or other dry red wine	1 pound fresh mushrooms, halved
2 bay leaves	6 cups hot cooked egg noodles or rice
2 tablespoons olive oil	

COMBINE first 3 ingredients in a large heavy-duty, zip-top plastic bag; turn bag to coat beef. Marinate in refrigerator 8 hours, turning bag occasionally. Drain beef, discarding marinade. Pat beef dry with paper towel, and set aside.

COMBINE 3 cups wine and bay leaves in a medium skillet; bring to a boil. Cook, uncovered, 20 minutes or until reduced to 1 cup; remove and discard bay leaves.

MEANWHILE, heat 2 tablespoons oil in a large skillet or Dutch oven over medium-high heat. Add beef, shallots, and garlic. Sauté until beef is browned; sprinkle with 1/2 teaspoon salt and 1/2 teaspoon pepper. Reduce heat to medium. Sprinkle flour over beef; cook, stirring constantly, 4 to 5 minutes.

POUR reduced wine mixture and beef broth over beef; bring to a boil. Cover, reduce heat, and simmer 15 minutes. Remove lid, and continue simmering, uncovered, 30 more minutes or until beef is tender.

MEANWHILE, heat butter in a skillet over medium heat. Add mushrooms; cook 5 minutes or until tender. Sprinkle with remaining 1/4 teaspoon salt and 1/4 teaspoon pepper. Stir mushrooms into beef mixture. Simmer 5 minutes. Serve over noodles. **Yield:** 8 servings.

*When meat is labeled "beef tips" at the market, the work of cutting the meat into cubes has already been done for you.

Winemaker's Notes: *Serve with Biltmore Estate Cabernet Sauvignon*

VEAL CHOPS AND ZUCCHINI WITH ROSEMARY

The rosemary skewers permeate the meat with intense rosemary flavor.

1	tablespoon plus 1 teaspoon grated lemon rind	4	(1^1/$_4$-inch-thick) boneless veal loin chops
2	tablespoons fresh lemon juice	4	(4-inch) woody rosemary branches with leaves
^{1}/$_3$	cup olive oil	2^1/$_2$	pounds zucchini, sliced diagonally into ^{1}/$_2$-inch-thick pieces
1	tablespoon minced fresh rosemary		
^{1}/$_2$	teaspoon salt		Cooking spray
^{1}/$_8$	teaspoon pepper		

COMBINE first 6 ingredients in a 13- x 9- x 2-inch baking dish. Stir well; set aside.

WRAP tail end of each chop flush against the loin portion; pierce a hole through the entire length of tail end and loin chop with a metal skewer. Skewer each chop through the pierced hole with a rosemary branch to secure. Place chops in dish with marinade; cover and marinate in refrigerator 3 hours, turning chops occasionally. Add zucchini to marinade the last hour.

REMOVE chops and zucchini from marinade, discarding marinade. Coat grill rack with cooking spray; place rack over medium-hot coals (350° to 400°). Place chops on rack, and grill, covered with grill lid, 8 to 9 minutes on each side or to desired degree of doneness. Grill zucchini, covered with grill lid, 8 to 10 minutes on each side or until tender. **Yield:** 4 servings.

Winemaker's Notes: Serve with Château Biltmore Claret

Everything's Coming Up Rosemary

*G*ive rosemary a permanent place in your garden and enjoy fresh clippings for use in recipes like our veal chops—the more you clip this herb the more it grows.

As a perennial, rosemary dies back during the winter but returns in spring. Preserve your herbal harvest during cold months by drying it: Invert a bundle in a brown paper bag, and hang in a cool dry place. After a couple of weeks when the stems are completely dry, remove herbs from the bag and store in an airtight container.

VEAL PICCATA

This classic main dish hails from Italy. Thin cutlets of veal, seasoned and dredged in flour, are quickly panfried until golden. Wine is added to deglaze the pan, and then the butter and lemon juice are added. The tangy sauce is drizzled over the veal just before serving. The results are outstanding in this simple recipe. You can even substitute boneless skinless chicken breasts (be sure to pound them) for the thin veal cutlets.

4 veal cutlets (about $^3/_4$ pound)

$^1/_4$ cup all-purpose flour

$^1/_2$ teaspoon salt

$^1/_2$ teaspoon pepper

2 tablespoons peanut or vegetable oil

$^1/_3$ cup Biltmore Estate Chardonnay Sur Lies or other dry white wine

2 tablespoons butter or margarine

2 tablespoons fresh lemon juice

2 teaspoons grated lemon rind

$^1/_4$ cup chopped fresh parsley

PLACE veal between two sheets of heavy-duty plastic wrap; flatten to $^1/_8$-inch thickness, using a meat mallet or rolling pin. Combine flour, salt, and pepper; dredge veal in flour mixture. Cook veal in oil in a large nonstick skillet over medium-high heat 1 minute on each side. Remove from skillet; keep warm.

ADD wine to hot skillet; cook over high heat, deglazing skillet by scraping bits that cling to bottom. Add butter and lemon juice; heat just until butter melts. Pour over veal, and sprinkle with lemon rind and parsley. **Yield:** 2 servings.

Winemaker's Notes: *Serve with Château Biltmore Cabernet Franc*

BUTTERFLIED LEG OF LAMB WITH MINT PESTO

1 (8-pound) leg of lamb, boned
   and butterflied

1 cup olive oil

1/4 cup loosely packed fresh basil
   leaves

3 tablespoons chopped fresh mint

2 tablespoons chopped fresh
   rosemary

5 cloves garlic, chopped

1 (750-milliliter) bottle
   Château Biltmore
   Cabernet Sauvignon or
   other dry red wine

1/2 teaspoon salt

1/4 teaspoon pepper

   Mint Pesto

TRIM fat from lamb. Place lamb in a large heavy-duty, zip-top plastic bag. Combine oil and next 5 ingredients in container of an electric blender; process until smooth, stopping once to scrape down sides. Pour oil mixture over lamb; seal bag, and turn until lamb is well coated. Marinate in refrigerator 8 hours, turning bag occasionally.

REMOVE lamb from marinade, discarding marinade. Sprinkle lamb with salt and pepper. Grill lamb, uncovered, over medium-hot coals (350° to 400°) 50 minutes or until a meat thermometer inserted in thickest portion of lamb registers 150° (medium rare) or to desired degree of doneness, turning once. Let lamb stand 15 minutes. Slice diagonally across grain into thin slices. Serve with Mint Pesto. **Yield:** 10 to 12 servings.

MINT PESTO

2 1/2 cups loosely packed fresh
   mint leaves

1 cup loosely packed fresh basil
   leaves

1/2 cup loosely packed flat-leaf
   parsley leaves

1 cup chopped walnuts

8 cloves garlic, cut in half

1 cup olive oil

1/2 teaspoon salt

1/4 teaspoon pepper

POSITION knife blade in food processor bowl; add first 5 ingredients. Process until finely chopped, stopping once to scrape down sides.

WITH processor running, pour oil in a thin, steady stream through food chute, processing just until smooth. Stir in salt and pepper. Cover and chill. **Yield:** about 2 cups.

Winemaker's Notes: *Serve with Château Biltmore Cabernet Sauvignon*

Lamb Chops with
Minted Apples

Bistro: Chef's Choice
LAMB CHOPS WITH MINTED APPLES

1 head garlic	Biltmore Dry Rub
1 tablespoon olive oil	Minted Apples
8 (2-inch-thick) lamb chops	

CUT off top of garlic head, and place on a piece of aluminum foil. Drizzle with olive oil, and fold foil to seal. Bake at 400° for 1 hour. Cool and peel 12 cloves, reserving any remaining cloves for other uses.

TRIM lamb chops. Sprinkle chops on both sides with desired amount of Biltmore Dry Rub, and place on a lightly greased rack in a broiler pan.

BAKE at 325° for 45 minutes or until a meat thermometer inserted into thickest portion registers 150° (medium rare). Reserve ¼ cup drippings for Minted Apples. Serve with Minted Apples and roasted garlic. **Yield:** 4 servings.

BILTMORE DRY RUB

3 cups salt	2 tablespoons garlic powder
2 tablespoons paprika	2 tablespoons pepper
2 tablespoons onion powder	1 tablespoon dried rosemary
2 tablespoons ground celery seeds	1 tablespoon ground sage
	1 tablespoon dried dillweed

STIR together all ingredients. **Yield:** about 4 cups.

MINTED APPLES

3 tablespoons butter	⅓ cup apple cider vinegar
2 shallots, thinly sliced	¼ cup reserved lamb drippings or bacon drippings
1 clove garlic, minced	2 tablespoons mint jelly
2 tablespoons sugar	2 teaspoons chopped fresh mint
3 Granny Smith apples, peeled and sliced	

MELT butter in a skillet over low heat. Add shallots and garlic; sauté until tender. Stir in sugar. Add apple; cook 3 minutes or until lightly caramelized, stirring often. Add vinegar, drippings, and jelly; cook 6 to 8 minutes, stirring often. Serve warm. Sprinkle with mint. **Yield:** 4 servings.

There's the Rub

A rub is a blend of dried herbs, spices, or other seasonings that is massaged onto the surface of a meat to infuse it with flavor. Since the coating remains on the food, the resulting flavor is intense. The Biltmore Dry Rub (recipe at left) can be used to season lamb, chicken, or steak, and it can be stored in an airtight container for up to six months.

CROWN ROAST OF PORK
WITH CHESTNUT STUFFING

For added flavor, substitute freshly roasted chestnuts for jar of chestnuts. Using 1 pound fresh chestnuts, cut a slit in each shell, and place on an ungreased baking sheet. Bake at 400° for 15 minutes; cool. Discard shells.

1 (16-rib) crown roast of pork (about 8 pounds)
1 tablespoon vegetable oil
1 teaspoon salt
$1/4$ teaspoon pepper
1 pound ground pork sausage
1 small onion, chopped (about $2/3$ cup)
$1/3$ cup chopped celery
1 clove garlic, minced
8 ounces French bread, cut into $1/2$-inch cubes ($5 1/2$ cups)

1 (11-ounce) jar shelled chestnuts, coarsely chopped
3 tablespoons chopped fresh parsley
1 teaspoon poultry seasoning
$1/2$ teaspoon dried thyme
$1/8$ teaspoon pepper
   Dash of salt
$1/2$ cup half-and-half
   Garnishes: lady apples, fresh thyme sprigs

BRUSH roast with oil; sprinkle on all sides with 1 teaspoon salt and $1/4$ teaspoon pepper. Place roast, bone ends up, in a shallow roasting pan. Insert meat thermometer, making sure it does not touch fat or bone. Bake at 475° for 15 minutes; reduce oven temperature to 325°, and bake 1 hour and 15 minutes.

MEANWHILE, brown sausage in a large nonstick skillet, stirring until it crumbles. Remove from skillet, reserving 1 tablespoon drippings in skillet; drain. Cook onion, celery, and garlic in skillet over medium-high heat, stirring constantly, until tender; remove from heat.

COMBINE sausage, onion mixture, bread cubes, and next 6 ingredients, mixing well. Pour half-and-half over stuffing, stirring gently until blended. Spoon 3 cups stuffing into center of roast, mounding slightly. Cover stuffing and exposed ends of ribs with aluminum foil; spoon remaining stuffing into a greased 11- x 7- x $1 1/2$-inch baking dish.

BAKE roast and dish of stuffing at 325° for 40 minutes or until thermometer registers 160°. Transfer roast to a large serving platter; remove foil. Let stand 10 minutes before carving. Garnish, if desired. **Yield:** 8 servings.

Winemaker's Notes: *Serve with Biltmore Estate Merlot*

GRILLED TERIYAKI PORK CHOPS
WITH SUMMER PEACH SALSA
(pictured on pages 2 and 74)

4 (6-ounce) center-cut pork chops (about ³/₄ inch thick)

¹/₄ cup soy sauce

3 tablespoons minced shallot

2 tablespoons Biltmore Estate Pinot Blanc or other dry white wine

2 tablespoons fresh lime juice

1 tablespoon minced, peeled fresh ginger

1¹/₂ teaspoons brown sugar

2 cloves garlic, minced
Summer Peach Salsa

TRIM fat from pork. Combine pork and next 7 ingredients in a large heavy-duty, zip-top plastic bag. Seal and marinate in refrigerator 4 hours, turning bag occasionally. Remove pork from bag, reserving marinade. Bring marinade to a boil; set aside.

GRILL pork, covered with grill lid, over medium-hot coals (350° to 400°) 7 minutes on each side or until done, basting frequently with reserved marinade. Serve with Summer Peach Salsa. **Yield:** 4 servings.

SUMMER PEACH SALSA

1 cup diced peaches

¹/₂ cup diced plums

¹/₄ cup minced shallot

3 tablespoons orange juice

2 tablespoons minced fresh parsley

1 teaspoon grated lime rind

2 tablespoons fresh lime juice

1¹/₂ tablespoons chopped, seeded jalapeño pepper

1 tablespoon minced fresh mint

1 tablespoon honey

1 teaspoon minced, peeled fresh ginger

COMBINE all ingredients in a bowl. Cover and chill. **Yield:** 2 cups.

Winemaker's Notes: Serve with Biltmore Estate Pinot Blanc

MARGARITA PORK KABOBS

Colorful green and red bell peppers and yellow corn flank the meat on these skewers, creating a visually pleasing entrée.

1 cup frozen margarita mix
    concentrate, thawed

1 teaspoon ground coriander

3 cloves garlic, minced

2 teaspoons grated lime rind

2 pounds pork tenderloin,
    cut into 1-inch cubes

3 ears fresh shucked corn

1 tablespoon water

1 large onion, quartered

1 large green bell pepper,
    cut into 1-inch pieces

1 large red bell pepper, cut
    into 1-inch pieces

COMBINE first 4 ingredients in a shallow dish; add pork. Cover; chill 30 minutes, turning occasionally.

CUT each ear of corn into 4 pieces. Place corn and 1 tablespoon water in an 8-inch square microwave-safe dish. Cover with heavy-duty plastic wrap, folding back 1 corner to allow steam to escape. Microwave at HIGH 4 minutes, giving dish a half turn after 2 minutes.

REMOVE pork from marinade, discarding marinade. Thread pork, corn, onion, and bell pepper pieces onto metal skewers.

GRILL kabobs, covered with grill lid, over medium-hot coals (350° to 400°) 5 minutes on each side or until done. **Yield:** 4 servings.

Winemaker's Notes: *Serve with Biltmore Estate Riesling*

Skewer Secrets

Consider serving these colorful skewers over a bed of couscous accented with fresh basil to complement the lime in the marinade. You'll find that cooking the corn slightly before grilling will aid in threading it on the skewer and hasten the cooking process.

TAWNY BAKED HAM

As it bakes, this succulent ham will whet eager appetites
with a smoky, sweet aroma.

1 (19-pound) smoked, fully
    cooked whole ham
1/3 cup Dijon mustard
1 cup firmly packed brown
    sugar
    About 2 teaspoons whole
    cloves
2 cups apple cider

2 cups pitted whole dates
2 cups dried figs, stems
    removed
2 cups pitted prunes
2 cups tawny port wine
    Garnishes: kumquats, dried
    figs, pineapple sage leaves

REMOVE and discard skin from ham. Score fat on ham in a diamond design. Brush mustard over top and sides of ham. Coat ham with brown sugar, pressing into mustard, if necessary.

USING an ice pick, make a hole in center of each diamond. Insert a clove into each hole. Place ham, fat side up, in a lightly greased large shallow roasting pan. Insert meat thermometer, making sure it does not touch fat or bone. Pour apple cider into pan. Bake, uncovered, at 350° for 2 hours, basting often with apple cider.

COMBINE dates and next 3 ingredients; pour into pan with ham. Bake 30 minutes or until meat thermometer registers 140°, basting often with mixture in pan; cover ham with aluminum foil to prevent overbrowning.

TRANSFER ham to a serving platter; let stand 10 minutes before slicing. Remove fruit from pan, using a slotted spoon, and set aside.

POUR pan drippings into a large saucepan, and cook over medium-high heat until reduced by half. Stir in reserved fruit. Serve sauce with ham. Garnish, if desired. **Yield:** 35 servings.

Winemaker's Notes: *Serve with Biltmore Estate Cerise*

Garlic-Rosemary Roasted Chicken with Potatoes

The beauty of roasted chicken is its versatility. Use the roasted garlic as a savory spread for French bread.

1 (5- to 6-pound) whole chicken	2 heads garlic
1 tablespoon chopped fresh rosemary	1½ pounds baking potatoes
8 cloves garlic, crushed	3 tablespoons olive oil
2 tablespoons olive oil, divided	¼ teaspoon salt
¼ teaspoon paprika	¼ teaspoon pepper
8 shallots or small onions	Garnish: fresh rosemary sprigs

LOOSEN skin from chicken breast and drumsticks by inserting fingers and gently pushing between the skin and meat. Place rosemary and crushed garlic beneath skin on breasts and drumsticks. Tie ends of legs together with string. Place chicken, breast side up, on a rack in a broiler pan. Brush chicken with 1 tablespoon olive oil, and sprinkle with paprika.

CUT a thin slice from each shallot. Remove skin, and cut off tops of garlic heads, leaving roots intact. Brush shallots and garlic with 1 tablespoon olive oil; arrange vegetables around chicken. Bake, uncovered, at 450° for 30 minutes.

MEANWHILE, cut potatoes lengthwise into thin strips. Combine potato strips and next 3 ingredients in a large heavy-duty, zip-top plastic bag. Seal bag, and shake to coat. Remove potato strips from bag, and arrange in a single layer on a baking sheet.

REDUCE temperature to 400°; add potatoes to lower oven rack. Bake chicken and potatoes at 400° for 35 minutes or until meat thermometer inserted in meaty part of thigh registers 180°, stirring potatoes after 15 minutes. Remove chicken from oven.

INCREASE oven temperature to Broil. Broil potatoes 5½ inches from heat 12 to 15 minutes or until crisp and golden, stirring frequently. Place chicken on a serving platter and serve with roasted garlic, shallots, and potatoes. Garnish, if desired. **Yield:** 6 to 8 servings.

Winemaker's Notes: Serve with Biltmore Estate Merlot

Garlic-Rosemary
Roasted Chicken
with Potatoes

SEASONED ROTISSERIE CHICKEN

This recipe makes enough seasoning for one chicken; however, you may want to double it to have enough on hand for another meal.

2	tablespoons seasoning salt	1/4	teaspoon dried oregano
2 1/4	teaspoons garlic powder	1/4	teaspoon dried parsley flakes
2 1/4	teaspoons onion powder	1/4	teaspoon paprika
1	teaspoon black pepper	1	(3- to 3 1/2-pound) broiler-fryer
1/4	teaspoon ground red pepper		
1/4	teaspoon dried basil	1	tablespoon olive oil

COMBINE first 9 ingredients in a bowl; stir well.

BRUSH chicken with olive oil; coat chicken with seasoning mixture. Place chicken, breast side up, on a greased rack in broiler pan or on a vertical roasting rack.

BAKE at 400° for 45 minutes or until meat thermometer inserted in meaty part of thigh registers 180°. **Yield:** 4 servings.

Winemaker's Notes: *Serve with Biltmore Estate Cardinal's Crest*

PECAN CHICKEN

*Buttery pecans roasted with the chicken lend crunch
to the rich Dijon-sour cream sauce that distinguishes this dish.*

8	skinned, boned chicken breast halves	1/4	cup plus 2 tablespoons Dijon mustard, divided
1/2	teaspoon salt	1	cup coarsely chopped pecans
1/8	teaspoon pepper	1	(16-ounce) carton sour cream
1/2	cup butter or margarine, melted	1/3	cup water (optional)

SPRINKLE chicken with salt and pepper; place in a greased 13- x 9- x 2-inch baking dish. Combine butter and 1/4 cup mustard; stir well. Pour over chicken; sprinkle pecans over top. Bake, uncovered, at 375° for 35 minutes or until chicken is done. Remove chicken to a serving platter, reserving drippings in dish; keep warm.

COMBINE remaining 2 tablespoons mustard, pan drippings, sour cream, and water, if desired, in a large saucepan; cook over medium heat until thoroughly heated, stirring often. To serve, pour sauce over chicken. **Yield:** 8 servings.

Winemaker's Notes: Serve with Château Biltmore Chardonnay

Bistro: Chef's Choice
CHICKEN WITH GORGONZOLA CREAM SAUCE FOR FRESH PASTA
Try this recipe over our Homemade Pasta, page 128.

4 skinned, boned chicken breast halves	$^1/_3$ cup crumbled Gorgonzola cheese
Dash of salt and pepper	1 to $1^1/_2$ tablespoons chopped fresh sage
$^1/_4$ cup all-purpose flour	$^1/_4$ teaspoon salt
1 tablespoon olive oil	$^1/_2$ teaspoon freshly ground pepper
2 shallots, minced	
2 cloves garlic, minced	Hot cooked fresh pasta
$^1/_2$ cup Château Biltmore Chardonnay or other dry white wine	Garnishes: fresh sage sprigs, crumbled Gorgonzola
3 cups heavy whipping cream	

PLACE chicken between two sheets of heavy-duty plastic wrap. Flatten to $^1/_4$-inch thickness, using a meat mallet or rolling pin. Sprinkle with salt and pepper; dredge in flour.

HEAT oil in a large skillet over medium-high heat until hot. Add chicken; sauté 8 minutes or until chicken is done, turning once. Remove chicken from pan; set aside, and keep warm.

REDUCE heat to medium; add shallot and garlic. Sauté 3 minutes. Add wine; cook over medium-high heat 2 minutes or until liquid reduces to about 3 tablespoons. Stir in cream; cook 5 minutes or until liquid reduces to about 2 cups. Stir in Gorgonzola, sage, $^1/_4$ teaspoon salt, and $^1/_2$ teaspoon pepper.

PLACE chicken over pasta; spoon sauce over top. Garnish with sage sprigs and crumbled Gorgonzola, if desired. **Yield:** 4 servings.

Winemaker's Notes: Serve with Château Biltmore Chardonnay

Marinade Magic

*M*arinades add a flavor punch to any meal, and their acid tenderizes tough cuts of meat.

• The size and consistency of foods determine the amount of time they need to marinate. Some foods take longer to absorb flavor, while over-marinating causes other foods to become soft and mushy. Delicate foods like fish should only marinate 1 to 3 hours; medium-size cuts like chops and steaks can take 4 to 8 hours. Large roasts, whole birds, and tough meats will need at least 8 hours and can marinate as long as 24 hours.

• A heavy-duty, zip-top plastic bag makes marinating simple. It takes up little space and is convenient to coat the food. Best of all, cleanup is easy—just throw the bag away.

• To allow more flavor penetration, pierce meat or poultry with a fork before adding marinade.

• Use just enough marinade to cover the food—1/3 cup to 1/2 cup per pound of meat is adequate. Turn meat occasionally to encourage even flavor absorption.

• Be sure to discard leftover marinade that's been in contact with raw meat. If you plan to baste the meat with marinade while cooking or if you serve it on the side, boil leftover marinade to kill harmful bacteria.

CHICKEN IN CABERNET MARINADE

The Cabernet Marinade's blend of spices adds distinctive flavor, and the wine helps tenderize the chicken. Its versatility enhances any poultry or meat.

1½ teaspoons coriander seeds, crushed

1½ teaspoons juniper berries, crushed

1½ teaspoons black peppercorns, crushed

½ cup chopped onion

1 head elephant garlic, minced

1 tablespoon minced peeled fresh ginger

1 tablespoon minced fresh rosemary

¾ cup Biltmore Cabernet Sauvignon or other dry red wine

2 tablespoons balsamic vinegar

4 skinned, boned chicken breast halves*

TOAST first 3 ingredients in a small dry skillet over medium heat 2 minutes or until fragrant. Add onion, garlic, ginger, and rosemary; cook, stirring constantly, 2 minutes or until mixture becomes very fragrant. Stir in wine and vinegar.

PLACE chicken breast halves in a large heavy-duty, zip-top plastic bag. Add marinade. Marinate in refrigerator 3 hours. Discard marinade. Grill chicken, covered, over medium-hot coals (350° to 400°) 5 minutes on each side or until chicken is done. **Yield:** 4 servings.

*You can substitute 2 (1-pound) pork tenderloins or 4 (1-inch-thick) lamb sirloin chops for chicken. Marinate pork up to 8 hours. Grill tenderloins, covered, 18 to 20 minutes or until a meat thermometer inserted into thickest part of tenderloin registers 160°, turning once. Cover and let stand 10 minutes before slicing. Marinate lamb chops up to 48 hours. Grill chops, covered, over medium coals (300° to 350°) 8 to 10 minutes on each side or to desired degree of doneness.

Winemaker's Notes: *Serve with Biltmore Estate Zinfandel Blanc de Noir*

FRIED CHICKEN SANDWICHES WITH FRESH CUCUMBER RÉMOULADE

4 skinned, boned chicken
   breast halves
3 teaspoons salt, divided
3 teaspoons pepper, divided
2 large eggs
½ cup evaporated milk
½ cup water

2 cups all-purpose flour
   Vegetable oil
4 kaiser rolls, split
4 leaves green leaf lettuce
4 tomato slices
   Fresh Cucumber Rémoulade

SPRINKLE chicken breast halves with 1½ teaspoons salt and 1½ teaspoons pepper; place in a shallow dish. Combine eggs, evaporated milk, and water; pour over chicken, turning pieces to coat. Let stand 5 minutes.

MEANWHILE, combine flour and remaining salt and pepper in a heavy-duty, zip-top plastic bag. Place chicken, 1 piece at a time, into bag; seal and shake to coat.

POUR oil to depth of 1 inch in a heavy 10- to 12-inch skillet; heat to 350°. Fry chicken in hot oil over medium heat 4 minutes on each side or until chicken is done. Drain chicken on paper towels.

PLACE a chicken breast half on bottom half of each roll; top with lettuce and tomato. Spread top halves of rolls with Fresh Cucumber Rémoulade; place on top of lettuce and tomato. **Yield:** 4 servings.

Stable Café: Chef's Choice
FRESH CUCUMBER RÉMOULADE

1 cup mayonnaise
¾ cup minced fresh flat-leaf
   parsley
½ English cucumber, diced
   (about 1 cup)
½ cup diced purple onion
¼ cup ketchup
1 tablespoon capers

1 tablespoon Dijon mustard
½ teaspoon minced garlic
½ teaspoon Worcestershire
   sauce
¼ teaspoon freshly ground
   black pepper
¼ teaspoon hot sauce
⅛ teaspoon ground red pepper

COMBINE all ingredients in a bowl; cover and chill. **Yield:** 2 cups.

Winemaker's Notes: *Serve with Biltmore Estate Zinfandel Blanc de Noir*

STUFFED CORNISH HENS
WITH PEACH SAUCE

Cornish hens are one of the smallest members of the poultry family,
weighing from one to two pounds. One bird is typically a serving.

4 (1- to 1$^1/_2$-pound) Cornish hens

1 cup Biltmore Estate Carolina Peach Preserves, divided*

$^3/_4$ cup butter or margarine, divided

2 cups white bread cubes, toasted

$^1/_2$ cup sliced celery

$^1/_4$ cup chopped green onions

$^1/_4$ cup chopped fresh parsley

2 to 3 tablespoons Biltmore Estate Riesling or other dry white wine

$^3/_4$ teaspoon dried marjoram or dried oregano, divided

$^1/_2$ teaspoon salt

$^1/_4$ teaspoon pepper

$^1/_4$ teaspoon dried basil

REMOVE giblets from hens; reserve for another use. Rinse hens thoroughly with cold water, and pat dry. Lift wingtips up and over back, and tuck under hens. Set hens aside.

COMBINE $^1/_2$ cup preserves and $^1/_4$ cup butter in a small saucepan; cook over medium heat until melted, stirring often.

COMBINE preserves mixture, bread cubes, and next 4 ingredients in a large bowl. Add $^1/_4$ teaspoon marjoram, salt, pepper, and basil; stir mixture well. Spoon bread cube mixture evenly into cavities of hens. Close cavities, and secure with wooden picks. Tie ends of legs together with string. Place hens, breast side up, on a lightly greased rack in a shallow roasting pan. Bake at 350° for 1 hour.

COMBINE remaining $^1/_2$ cup preserves, $^1/_2$ cup butter, and $^1/_2$ teaspoon marjoram in a small saucepan. Cook over medium heat until melted, stirring often. Remove hens from oven, and brush with $^1/_2$ cup preserves mixture. Bake 30 more minutes or until done. Serve hens with remaining preserves mixture. **Yield:** 4 servings.

*You can substitute Biltmore Estate Carolina Peaches and Brandy Preserves or apricot preserves, if desired.

Winemaker's Notes: *Serve with Biltmore Estate Merlot*

HOLIDAY TURKEY

Marinating the turkey at least 6 hours before cooking infuses the meat with more flavor than simply sprinkling on the seasonings and immediately baking the bird. The sweet vermouth sauce ensures a tender entrée.

1	(10- to 12-pound) turkey	1	cup chopped onion
2	tablespoons salt	1½	cups sweet vermouth
1	tablespoon pepper	½	cup honey
⅓	cup balsamic vinegar		Garnishes: fresh parsley
1	tablespoon minced garlic		sprigs, kumquat leaves,
2	tablespoons olive oil		kumquats

REMOVE giblets and neck from turkey, and reserve for another use. Rinse turkey with cold water, and pat dry.

PLACE turkey in a large shallow dish. Stir together 2 tablespoons salt and next 4 ingredients; pour mixture over turkey. Cover turkey, and chill at least 6 hours.

REMOVE turkey from refrigerator, and brush turkey cavity with marinade. Lift wingtips up and over back, and tuck them under bird. Place turkey, breast side up, in a large greased roasting pan. Cover turkey with aluminum foil, and bake at 400° for 30 minutes. Reduce heat to 350°, and bake 2 hours, basting occasionally with pan drippings.

PROCESS 1 cup onion, vermouth, and honey in container of an electric blender until smooth. Pour mixture over turkey, and bake 1 more hour or until a meat thermometer inserted into turkey thigh registers 180°.

BROIL turkey 5½ inches from heat until golden. Garnish, if desired. **Yield:** 10 to 12 servings.

Winemaker's Notes: *Serve with Biltmore Estate Claret*

Thawing the Bird

*I*f you purchase a frozen turkey, it's important to thaw it properly before cooking. The best way to let a turkey thaw is in the refrigerator—and this may take several days depending on the weight of the bird. Thawing it in the refrigerator instead of at room temperature is the safest method to use because it reduces the risk of bacterial growth.

Leave the turkey in its original wrapping, place it in a pan to catch any juices, and refrigerate until thawed. Allow two to four days for thawing. A 4- to 12-pound bird will take one to two days to thaw; a 12- to 20-pound bird will take two to three days; and a 20- to 24-pound turkey will take up to four days to thaw. Once thawed, a turkey should be cooked immediately.

TURKEY SCALOPPINE
Scaloppine refers to thin scallops or slices of meat, usually accompanied by a sauce.

1¹/₂ pounds turkey tenderloins, cut in half horizontally	3 tablespoons butter or margarine, divided
¹/₂ teaspoon salt	Hot cooked fettuccine
¹/₂ teaspoon pepper	Sage Beurre Blanc
³/₄ cup all-purpose flour	

PLACE turkey between 2 sheets of heavy-duty plastic wrap, and flatten to ¹/₄-inch thickness using a meat mallet or rolling pin. Sprinkle turkey with salt and pepper, and dredge in flour.

HEAT 1¹/₂ tablespoons butter in a large skillet over medium heat. Add half of turkey; cook 4 minutes on each side or until done and lightly browned. Set aside, and keep warm. Repeat procedure with remaining turkey.

ARRANGE turkey over fettuccine on a warm serving platter. Spoon Sage Beurre Blanc over turkey and pasta. **Yield:** 4 servings.

SAGE BEURRE BLANC

1 cup cold unsalted butter	¹/₃ cup champagne vinegar
¹/₂ cup chopped shallot	1 cup heavy whipping cream
¹/₂ cup fresh sage leaves, stems reserved	¹/₂ teaspoon salt
¹/₄ cup Biltmore Estate Chenin Blanc or other sweet white wine	¹/₄ teaspoon ground white pepper

CUT butter into 1-inch cubes. Heat 1 cube butter in a saucepan over medium-high heat; add shallot and sage stems. Cook, stirring, 30 seconds. Stir in wine and vinegar; simmer until liquid reduces by half. Stir in cream; bring to a simmer. Reduce heat to low. Gradually add remaining butter, stirring constantly with a wire whisk, until all butter is incorporated.

STRAIN mixture through a fine wire-mesh strainer into a bowl, discarding solids; stir in salt and pepper. Chop sage leaves; stir into sauce. Serve immediately. **Yield:** 2 cups.

Winemaker's Notes: *Serve with Biltmore Estate Pinot Noir*

Bistro: Chef's Choice

OVEN-ROASTED ESTATE TROUT WITH PECAN CRUST AND MEUNIÈRE BUTTER

The richness of the pecans and lemon butter sauce provides an elegant contrast to the mild flavor of fresh trout.

2 pounds rainbow trout fillets	$1/4$ cup butter
$1/2$ teaspoon salt	1 tablespoon chopped fresh parsley
$1/4$ teaspoon ground white pepper	
1 tablespoon butter	2 tablespoons fresh lemon juice
Pecan Crust	

SPRINKLE trout with salt and pepper.

HEAT 1 tablespoon butter in a cast-iron skillet over medium-high heat until hot. Place 2 trout fillets in skillet; sear 3 minutes. Turn over; top each trout with about $1/4$ cup Pecan Crust. Broil $5^1/2$ inches from heat (with electric oven door partially opened) 3 to 4 minutes or until browned. Transfer to a platter; keep warm. Repeat process with remaining trout.

HEAT $1/4$ cup butter in a small saucepan over medium-high heat. Cook until lightly brown. Add parsley and lemon juice. Transfer trout to individual serving plates; drizzle with butter sauce. **Yield:** 4 servings.

PECAN CRUST

$1^1/4$ cups pecans, ground	1 tablespoon chopped fresh mint
$1/2$ cup soft breadcrumbs (homemade)	
	1 tablespoon fresh lemon juice
2 tablespoons olive oil	$1/4$ teaspoon salt
1 tablespoon chopped fresh basil	$1/4$ teaspoon ground white pepper

COMBINE all ingredients in a medium bowl. **Yield:** $1^1/2$ cups.

Winemaker's Notes: *Serve with Château Biltmore Chardonnay*

Trout Amandine

TROUT AMANDINE

You'll need to cook the fish in batches. To keep warm, place cooked fish on a wire rack in a shallow pan. Then place the pan in a 200° oven.

2	tablespoons butter	1	teaspoon pepper
1/3	cup sliced almonds	6	(12-ounce) rainbow trout fillets
1/2	cup milk		Vegetable oil
1	egg yolk		Lemon Cream Sauce
1/2	teaspoon hot sauce		Garnish: lemon wedges
1	cup all-purpose flour		
1	teaspoon salt		

MELT butter in a large heavy skillet over low heat; add almonds, and sauté until golden. Remove almonds from skillet; drain on paper towels. Wipe skillet clean.

WHISK together milk, egg yolk, and hot sauce in a shallow dish. Stir together flour, salt, and pepper in a bowl. Dredge fillets in flour mixture; dip in egg mixture. Dredge fillets again in flour mixture, shaking to remove excess flour mixture.

POUR oil to a depth of 1/4 inch into skillet; heat to 375°. Fry trout in batches 3 to 4 minutes on each side or until golden. Serve with Lemon Cream Sauce; sprinkle with almonds. Garnish, if desired. **Yield:** 6 servings.

LEMON CREAM SAUCE

1/2	cup butter	1/3	cup whipping cream
2	tablespoons all-purpose flour	1/4	cup white wine Worcestershire sauce
1	(14 1/2-ounce) can chicken broth	1/4	teaspoon salt
2	cloves garlic, pressed	1/2	teaspoon hot sauce
1	tablespoon lemon juice		

MELT butter in a large skillet over medium heat; whisk in flour. Cook, whisking constantly, 1 minute. Whisk in broth, garlic, and lemon juice; bring to a boil, whisking constantly. Reduce heat, and simmer, whisking constantly, 5 minutes. Whisk in whipping cream and remaining ingredients, and cook, whisking constantly, 5 minutes or until thickened. **Yield:** 1 1/4 cups.

Winemaker's Notes: *Serve with Château Biltmore Chardonnay*

SHRIMP SCAMPI

2 pounds unpeeled jumbo fresh
   shrimp

8 ounces dried linguine

8 cloves garlic, minced

1 cup butter or margarine,
   melted

1 cup Biltmore Estate
   Sauvignon Blanc or other
   dry white wine

1/4 teaspoon salt

1/8 teaspoon pepper

1/4 cup chopped fresh parsley

PEEL shrimp, leaving tails intact; devein, if desired. Cook linguine according to package directions; drain and keep warm.

COOK garlic in butter and wine in a large skillet over medium heat, stirring constantly, 4 minutes or until garlic begins to brown. Add shrimp, and cook over medium heat 3 to 5 minutes or until shrimp turn pink. Add salt and pepper, and spoon mixture over linguine. Sprinkle with chopped parsley, and serve immediately. **Yield:** 4 servings.

Winemaker's Notes: Serve with Biltmore Estate Blanc de Blanc-Brut

Powerful Poblanos

*T*he poblano pepper is considered the workhorse of southwestern cooking because of its versatility. This medium to hot pepper resembles an elongated green bell pepper, and is good for stuffing. Roasted poblanos are especially delicious.

POBLANO PEPPER SHRIMP

1 pound unpeeled medium-size
   fresh shrimp

2 small poblano peppers

1/2 cup unsalted butter, divided

2 cloves garlic, minced

2 tablespoons chopped fresh
   basil

2 cups diced tomato

1 cup chopped onion

1/2 teaspoon salt

1/4 teaspoon black pepper

1 jalapeño pepper, seeded and
   chopped

1/4 cup chopped fresh cilantro

1 tablespoon fresh lime juice

PEEL shrimp, and devein, if desired; set aside.

CUT poblano peppers in half lengthwise; remove and discard seeds. Place peppers, skin side up, on an ungreased baking sheet; flatten peppers with palm of hand. Broil peppers 5 1/2 inches from heat 5 to 10 minutes or until charred. Place peppers in a heavy-duty, zip-top plastic bag; seal bag and let stand 10 minutes to loosen skins. Peel peppers, and discard skins. Cut peppers into thin strips; set aside.

MELT ¹/₄ cup butter in a large skillet over medium-high heat; add garlic. Cook 1 minute, stirring constantly. Add shrimp; cook 1 minute, stirring constantly. Add basil; cook 2 minutes or until shrimp turn pink, stirring occasionally. Transfer shrimp mixture to a bowl; set aside, and keep warm.

MELT remaining ¹/₄ cup butter in skillet over medium-high heat; add pepper strips, tomato, and next 4 ingredients. Cook, stirring constantly, 4 minutes or until tender. Stir in shrimp, cilantro, and lime juice; cook 2 minutes or until thoroughly heated. Serve immediately. **Yield:** 4 servings.

GRILLED ORANGE SCALLOPS WITH CILANTRO-LIME VINAIGRETTE

1 cup orange juice	Cilantro-Lime Vinaigrette
3 tablespoons chopped fresh basil	30 yellow pear tomatoes
18 sea scallops	30 red pear tomatoes or small cherry tomatoes
1 head Bibb lettuce, torn	2 cucumbers, cut into thin strips
4 cups mixed baby salad greens	

COMBINE orange juice and basil in a dish; add scallops, tossing to coat. Cover and chill about 1 hour.

REMOVE scallops, discarding marinade. Grill scallops, covered with grill lid, over hot coals (400° to 500°) 3 to 5 minutes on each side or until done.

DRIZZLE lettuce and baby salad greens with vinaigrette, and toss gently. Arrange on individual plates, and top evenly with scallops, tomatoes, and cucumber. Serve immediately. **Yield:** 6 servings.

CILANTRO-LIME VINAIGRETTE

¹/₄ cup sugar	1 clove garlic, minced
¹/₄ cup extra-virgin olive oil	1 shallot, minced
2 tablespoons lime juice	1¹/₂ teaspoons minced fresh cilantro leaves
2 tablespoons rice wine vinegar	

COMBINE all ingredients in a jar; cover tightly, and shake vigorously. **Yield:** ³/₄ cup.

Winemaker's Notes: Serve with Biltmore Estate Sauvignon Blanc

DOVES MERLOT

You won't find dove at the supermarket. However, if you're the lucky recipient of a hunter's catch, this moist-heat recipe with rich wine gravy will show off your fare. When cooking dove, remember the key is not to overcook the dark meat.

1 cup all-purpose flour	1 (10½-ounce) can beef consommé
1 teaspoon salt	
1 teaspoon cracked black pepper	½ cup Biltmore Estate Merlot or other dry red wine
12 doves, dressed	
⅓ cup butter	Hot cooked egg noodles or rice
1 small onion, chopped	
1 stalk celery, chopped	
1 small green bell pepper, chopped	

COMBINE first 3 ingredients in a large heavy-duty, zip-top plastic bag. Add doves, a few at a time; seal bag, and shake to coat.

MELT butter in a large nonstick skillet over medium-high heat; add doves, and cook until browned, turning once.

PLACE doves in a lightly greased 13- x 9- x 2-inch baking dish. Sprinkle vegetables evenly over doves; add consommé. Cover dish with aluminum foil.

BAKE at 350° for 1½ hours. Pour wine over doves; cover and bake 30 more minutes. Serve with noodles or rice. **Yield:** 6 servings.

Winemaker's Notes: *Serve with Biltmore Estate Merlot*

GRILLED QUAIL WITH RED WINE-BLACKBERRY SAUCE

Domestic quail are mild-flavored and lean game birds; wild quail have a subtle gamey taste. Allow two small birds per person. Look for domestic quail in the frozen meat section at the supermarket.

2 (14-ounce) packages quail, dressed with breasts deboned	½ cup Château Biltmore Pinot Noir or other dry red wine
1 cup Biltmore Estate Vidalia Onion Vinaigrette*	1 (12-ounce) jar Biltmore Estate Wild Blackberry Jam

RINSE quail, and pat dry. Place in a large shallow dish or heavy-duty zip-top, plastic bag; add vinaigrette. Cover or seal, and chill 8 hours. Remove quail, discarding marinade.

COOK wine in a small saucepan over medium heat 5 minutes or until reduced by half. Whisk in blackberry jam until smooth. Reserve $^3/_4$ cup.

GRILL quail, uncovered, over medium coals (300° to 350°) 15 minutes, turning once and basting with remaining blackberry sauce. Serve with reserved $^3/_4$ cup sauce. **Yield:** 4 servings.

*You can substitute 1 (8-ounce) bottle Italian dressing, if desired.

Winemaker's Notes: *Serve with Château Biltmore Pinot Noir*

ROASTED VEGETABLE PIZZA
Roasting the vegetables before using them as a topping develops a sweet, caramelized taste. You'll enjoy the extra flavor this effort produces.

1 (10-ounce) can refrigerated pizza crust dough
  Cooking spray
1 small sweet onion, cut into thin wedges
1 tablespoon chopped fresh or 1 teaspoon dried thyme
2 tablespoons balsamic vinegar
1 teaspoon olive oil
$^1/_4$ teaspoon salt

4 small red potatoes, cut into 8 wedges
4 cloves garlic, thinly sliced
1 small yellow squash, thinly sliced
1 small red bell pepper, cut into 2-inch pieces
$1^1/_4$ cups (5 ounces) shredded sharp provolone cheese

UNROLL pizza crust on a baking sheet coated with cooking spray; fold edges of dough to form an 11-inch circle. Bake at 425° for 7 minutes, and set aside.

TOSS together onion and next 8 ingredients; spoon into a 13- x 9- x 2-inch pan. Bake at 500° for 20 minutes, stirring once.

SPRINKLE half of provolone cheese over crust. Top with roasted vegetable mixture, and sprinkle evenly with remaining half of cheese.

BAKE at 425° for 10 minutes or until pizza crust is lightly browned and cheese is melted. Cut into wedges, and serve immediately. **Yield:** 6 servings.

Pasta Primer

*P*asta purists maintain that there's a world of difference between the flavor and texture of homemade pasta versus store-bought. Try our helpful hints below and judge for yourself.

• *The difference between brands of flour (and how much moisture they absorb) accounts for the range in flour and water. Start with the minimum amount of flour and water; if the dough seems too dry, add a few more drops of water. If too sticky, knead in a dusting of extra flour.*

• *Use a pastry brush to brush dough sheets with flour on both sides after the first pass in the pasta machine.*

• *Pass each dough sheet through the cutting rollers of the pasta machine. Two pairs of hands are helpful here.*

HOMEMADE PASTA

Fresh flavor, supple texture, and quick cooking are some of the benefits of making fresh pasta. Our photos of Basil Pasta at left guide you step by step.

3 to 4 cups semolina flour*	1/4 teaspoon salt
6 large eggs, lightly beaten	1/4 cup water

PLACE 3 cups flour in a bowl; make a well in center. Combine eggs, salt, and water; pour into center of flour well. Whisk wet ingredients with a fork, gradually stirring in flour from bottom of well; continue until blended and stiff. On a floured surface, knead dough by hand, dusting with more flour if dough becomes sticky. Knead until dough is no longer sticky and springs back when pressed in center. Cover and let rest 1 hour.

DIVIDE dough into thirds. Working with one portion of dough at a time and keeping reserved dough covered to prevent drying, pass dough through smooth rollers of pasta machine on widest setting. Brush dough with flour, using a pastry brush if dough becomes sticky; fold dough in half, and brush both sides lightly with flour. Repeat rolling through widest setting until dough is no longer sticky. Repeat procedure for settings 2 through 6 on pasta machine.

PASS each dough sheet through cutting rollers (cut sheet in half, crosswise, if it is too long to handle). Hang pasta on a wooden drying rack, clean wooden coat hangers, or a broom handle balanced between two chairs. Let pasta dry no longer than 30 minutes before cooking.

COMBINE 4 quarts of water and 2 teaspoons salt in a Dutch oven; bring to a boil. Add pasta; cook 2 to 3 minutes or until al dente. **Yield:** 12 cups.

*You can substitute 3½ to 4½ cups bread flour for semolina flour.

Fresh Basil Pasta: Add 3 tablespoons chopped fresh basil to egg, salt, and water mixture before blending.

Black Pepper Pasta: Add 2 tablespoons freshly ground black pepper to egg mixture before blending.

Spinach Pasta: Thaw, drain, and puree 1 (10-ounce) package frozen chopped spinach. Press 4 tablespoons spinach puree through a fine mesh sieve. Add to egg mixture before blending. (Reserve remaining spinach puree for another use.)

ROASTED VEGETABLE LASAGNA

For the most flavor, use a sharp, potent cheese in the filling.
Provolone, Parmesan, Romano, Asiago, or sharp Cheddar all work well.
Stick to mozzarella for the top, however, as it melts and browns the best.

4 red bell peppers, halved and seeded

1 teaspoon olive oil

½ teaspoon salt

½ teaspoon black pepper

6 yellow squash, halved lengthwise and cut into 1-inch pieces (about 1½ pounds)

1 large onion, cut into 16 wedges

4 cloves garlic, minced

2 cups cottage cheese

1½ cups (6 ounces) grated sharp provolone cheese

¼ cup chopped fresh basil

1 teaspoon dried oregano

3 tablespoons all-purpose flour

1½ cups milk

2 tablespoons chopped fresh basil

¼ teaspoon black pepper

9 cooked lasagna noodles

2 cups spinach leaves, divided

½ cup (2 ounces) shredded part-skim mozzarella cheese

Garnish: fresh basil sprigs

PLACE pepper halves, skin sides up, on a baking sheet; flatten with palm of hand. Broil 5½ inches from heat 5 to 10 minutes or until charred. Place in a zip-top plastic bag; seal. Let stand 15 minutes. Peel and discard skins, and set aside.

COMBINE oil, salt, ½ teaspoon black pepper, squash, and onion on a baking sheet; toss well. Bake at 450° for 20 minutes. Remove from oven; combine squash mixture and garlic in bowl; set aside.

COMBINE cottage cheese and next 3 ingredients in a bowl; set aside.

PLACE flour in a medium saucepan. Gradually add 1½ cups milk; stir with a wire whisk. Place over medium heat. Cook until thick, stirring sauce constantly. Remove from heat; stir in 2 tablespoons chopped basil and ¼ teaspoon black pepper.

SPREAD ¼ cup white sauce in bottom of a lightly greased 13- x 9- x 2-inch baking dish. Arrange 3 noodles over sauce; top with 1¼ cups cheese mixture, 1 cup spinach, 4 bell pepper halves, 2 cups vegetable mixture, and ¼ cup white sauce. Repeat layers, ending with noodles. Spread remaining white sauce over noodles. Cover and bake at 375° for 15 minutes. Uncover; sprinkle with mozzarella cheese. Bake 20 more minutes. Garnish, if desired.
Yield: 9 servings.

EGGPLANT TIMBALES WITH RATATOUILLE

*Making the ratatouille a day ahead saves a step in preparing this elegant
vegetarian entrée. If you've got time, make the homemade Marinara Sauce
on page 65, instead of using store-bought, for a well-worth-the-effort dinner.*

2	medium eggplants	$1/4$	teaspoon black pepper
2	large eggs, beaten		Ratatouille
$1^1/2$	cups all-purpose flour	3	cups (12 ounces) shredded
	Vegetable oil		mozzarella cheese
$1/4$	teaspoon salt	$1^1/2$	cups marinara sauce, warmed

PEEL eggplant, if desired. Cut into 36 ($1/4$-inch) slices, reserving remaining
eggplant for other uses. Dip sliced eggplant in egg; dredge in flour. Pour oil to
depth of $1/2$ inch in a large skillet. Fry eggplant in hot oil until golden on each
side; drain on paper towels. Sprinkle eggplant with salt and pepper.

LINE six 10-ounce lightly greased custard cups with 5 eggplant slices, 1 on the
bottom and 4 around sides, overlapping slices if necessary. Combine Ratatouille
and cheese; stir well. Fill each eggplant-lined cup with 1 cup ratatouille mixture;
top with 1 eggplant slice. Bake at 350° for 25 minutes; let stand 5 minutes. Invert
onto individual plates. Serve with marinara sauce. **Yield:** 6 servings.

RATATOUILLE

2	tablespoons olive oil	1	medium zucchini, diced
1	small eggplant, peeled and		(about $1^1/2$ cups)
	diced	$3/4$	teaspoon salt
1	green bell pepper, diced	$1/2$	teaspoon black pepper
	(about $1^1/3$ cups)	1	cup marinara sauce
$1/2$	purple onion, diced	1	teaspoon minced garlic
	(about $1^1/4$ cups)	$1/4$	teaspoon fresh thyme

HEAT oil in a large skillet until very hot. Add eggplant; sauté 3 minutes
or until slightly tender. Stir in bell pepper and onion; reduce heat and cook,
stirring often, 5 minutes. Stir in zucchini, salt, and pepper; cook, stirring
often, 7 minutes or until zucchini is tender. Stir in marinara sauce, garlic, and
thyme; cook, stirring often, until well blended and thick. **Yield:** $3^1/2$ cups.

Winemaker's Notes: *Serve with Biltmore Estate Chardonnay Sur Lies*

SALADS & SIDES

Fresh Mozzarella-
Tomato-Basil Salad, page 132

CITRUS SALAD WITH HONEY VINAIGRETTE

4 navel oranges, peeled and
   sliced crosswise
2 pink grapefruit, peeled and
   sectioned
2 ripe avocados, peeled and
   sliced

½ cup thinly sliced purple
   onion
Bibb lettuce leaves
3 tablespoons pine nuts or
   walnuts, toasted
Honey Vinaigrette

ARRANGE first 4 ingredients evenly on six individual lettuce-lined salad plates. Sprinkle with pine nuts, and drizzle with Honey Vinaigrette. **Yield:** 6 servings.

HONEY VINAIGRETTE

⅓ cup vegetable oil
⅓ cup cranberry juice drink
2 tablespoons honey

1 tablespoon raspberry vinegar
   or red wine vinegar
1 teaspoon grated orange rind

COMBINE all ingredients in a jar; cover tightly, and shake vigorously. **Yield:** ¾ cup.

FRESH MOZZARELLA-TOMATO-BASIL SALAD

Fresh mozzarella is a soft white cheese available at gourmet grocery stores or cheese shops. Sometimes it's packed in a solution of water and salt used for preserving foods. See the salad on page 131.

½ pound fresh mozzarella
   cheese
2 large red tomatoes, sliced
1 large yellow tomato, sliced
½ teaspoon salt

½ cup fresh basil leaves
3 tablespoons extra-virgin
   olive oil
Freshly ground pepper
Garnish: fresh basil leaves

REMOVE cheese from brine, and cut into 12 slices; sprinkle tomato slices evenly with salt. Alternate 4 tomato slices, 3 cheese slices, and 3 basil leaves in a stack. Repeat with remaining tomato slices, cheese slices, and basil leaves. Drizzle with olive oil. Cover and chill 4 hours. Just before serving, sprinkle with freshly ground pepper. Garnish, if desired. **Yield:** 4 servings.

ROMAINE CHIFFONADE WITH PESTO VINAIGRETTE

1 purple onion	1 tablespoon minced garlic
8 cups shredded romaine lettuce	¼ cup balsamic vinegar
2 tablespoons pine nuts	½ teaspoon salt
2 tablespoons chopped fresh basil	½ teaspoon cracked black pepper
	½ cup olive oil

CUT onion into thin slices, and separate into rings. Combine onion and lettuce in a large bowl.

PROCESS pine nuts and next 5 ingredients in a blender until smooth, stopping once to scrape down sides. Turn blender on high; add oil in a slow, steady stream. Pour over lettuce and onion; toss gently. Serve immediately.
Yield: 8 servings.

Stable Café: Chef's Choice

BILTMORE VINAIGRETTE DRESSING

Whirl these ingredients with a wire whisk to make a thin vinaigrette, or use an electric blender for a thick, creamy dressing. To blend, process first 9 ingredients in a blender or food processor; gradually add oil by pouring it through the food chute.

1 tablespoon egg substitute*	¼ teaspoon salt
¼ cup cider vinegar	¼ teaspoon paprika
¼ cup spicy mustard	⅛ teaspoon ground white pepper
½ tablespoon Worcestershire sauce	1 clove garlic, chopped
½ teaspoon sugar	1 cup vegetable oil

COMBINE first 9 ingredients in a small bowl; stir with a wire whisk until blended. Gradually add oil, whisking constantly. Serve over salad greens.
Yield: 1½ cups.

*The FDA does not recommend substituting raw egg for the egg substitute.

ANGEL HAIR PASTA WITH PESTO

Pesto makes the most of fresh basil. Try it on grilled foods such as fish or chicken,
or as a base for your homemade pizza or potato salad.

2 cups firmly packed fresh
   basil leaves

2 cloves garlic

3 tablespoons pine nuts, lightly
   toasted

⅓ cup freshly grated Parmesan
   cheese

⅓ cup olive oil

½ teaspoon salt

6 ounces uncooked dried angel
   hair pasta

PROCESS first 6 ingredients in a food processor or an electric blender
1 minute or until smooth, stopping once to scrape down sides.

COOK pasta according to package directions; drain. Spoon pesto mixture
over pasta; toss gently, and serve immediately. **Yield:** 6 servings.

Winemaker's Notes: *Serve with Biltmore Estate Cabernet Blanc de Noir*

CRACKED PEPPER LINGUINE

8 ounces uncooked dried
   linguine

1 tablespoon butter

¼ cup minced onion

2 cloves garlic, pressed

1 (8-ounce) carton sour cream

1 tablespoon milk

2 to 3 teaspoons cracked black
   pepper

2 tablespoons freshly grated
   Parmesan cheese

2 tablespoons chopped fresh
   parsley

Garnish: fresh parsley sprigs

COOK pasta according to package directions; drain and keep warm.

MELT butter in a small skillet over medium-high heat; add onion and
garlic, and sauté until crisp-tender. Remove mixture from heat, and cool
slightly.

STIR in sour cream, milk, and pepper. Toss with pasta. Sprinkle with
cheese and chopped parsley. Garnish, if desired. **Yield:** 4 servings.

Winemaker's Notes: *Serve with Biltmore Estate Cerise*

Pasta with Asparagus, Prosciutto, and Wild Mushrooms

Brie adds buttery goodness to a medley of fresh asparagus, salty prosciutto, and meaty shiitake mushrooms.

1 (16-ounce) package dried
    spaghetti, uncooked

1 teaspoon olive oil

1 pound fresh asparagus spears

¼ cup diced shallot

2 tablespoons minced garlic

¼ cup olive oil

3 ounces prosciutto, cut into
    thin strips

1 (3½-ounce) package shiitake
    mushrooms, sliced

1 cup chicken broth

⅓ cup Château Biltmore
    Chardonnay or other dry
    white wine

½ teaspoon salt

¼ teaspoon pepper

4 ounces Brie cheese, cut into
    thin slices

COOK spaghetti according to package directions; drain. Add 1 teaspoon olive oil; toss. Set spaghetti aside, and keep warm.

MEANWHILE, snap off tough ends of asparagus. Remove scales with a vegetable peeler, if desired. Cut asparagus into 1-inch pieces. Set aside.

COOK shallot and minced garlic in ¼ cup olive oil in a large skillet over medium-high heat, stirring constantly, until golden. Add asparagus and prosciutto. Cook 3 minutes, stirring constantly. Add mushrooms; cook 5 minutes, stirring constantly. Add broth, wine, salt, and pepper; cook 2 minutes, stirring constantly.

COMBINE prosciutto mixture and reserved spaghetti in a large bowl, and toss gently. Add cheese slices, and toss gently. Serve immediately. **Yield:** 6 servings.

Winemaker's Notes: *Serve with Château Biltmore Chardonnay*

ORANGE HERB RICE

2 tablespoons chopped onion

2 tablespoons butter or
    margarine, melted

2 cups water

1/2 teaspoon grated orange rind

1/2 cup fresh orange juice

1 teaspoon salt

1/8 teaspoon dried marjoram

1/8 teaspoon dried thyme

1 cup uncooked long-grain rice

COOK onion in butter in a large saucepan over medium-high heat, stirring constantly, until tender. Add water and next 5 ingredients; bring to a boil. Stir in rice. Cover, reduce heat, and simmer 25 minutes or until rice is tender and liquid is absorbed. **Yield:** 6 to 8 servings.

WILD RICE-VEGETABLE MEDLEY

To turn this into a quick and easy entrée, stir in 1 cup chopped cooked chicken.

1 tablespoon olive oil

1 cup chopped green bell pepper

3/4 cup chopped onion

3/4 cup finely chopped carrot

1 (8-ounce) package sliced
    fresh mushrooms

1 (2 3/4-ounce) package instant
    wild rice, uncooked

1 1/3 cups chicken broth

1/4 teaspoon salt

1/4 teaspoon black pepper

Garnish: fresh flat-leaf
    parsley leaves

HEAT oil over medium-high heat until hot. Add bell pepper and next 3 ingredients; sauté until carrot is tender.

ADD rice and broth. Bring to a boil; reduce heat. Simmer, uncovered, 5 minutes or until liquid is absorbed. Stir in salt and pepper. Let stand 5 minutes. Garnish with parsley, if desired. **Yield:** 5 servings.

Winemaker's Notes: *Serve with Biltmore Estate Chardonnay Sur Lies*

PISTACHIO RISOTTO WITH SAFFRON

¼ cup unsalted butter	5 cups chicken broth, divided
1 medium-size yellow onion, chopped	1 cup freshly grated Parmesan cheese
1 teaspoon saffron threads	3 tablespoons coarsely chopped pistachios
1¾ cups uncooked Arborio rice	
1 cup dry white vermouth	

MELT butter in a skillet over medium-high heat; add onion, and sauté 5 minutes. Add saffron; sauté 1 minute. Add rice; cook, stirring constantly, 2 minutes. Reduce heat to medium; add vermouth and 2 cups broth. Cook, stirring constantly, until liquid is absorbed.

REPEAT procedure with remaining broth, ½ cup at a time, until liquid is absorbed. (Cooking time is 30 to 45 minutes.) Remove from heat; stir in cheese and pistachios. **Yield:** 8 cups.

Stable Café: Chef's Choice
GREEN TOMATO RELISH

This "relish" may remind you of a fresh salsa. Serve it over fish or chicken or as a colorful dip for tortilla chips. The standing time intensifies the fresh flavor.

2 medium-size red tomatoes, diced (about 2½ cups)	Grated rind of 1 lemon (about 2 tablespoons)
1 medium-size green tomato, diced (about 1¼ cups)	Juice of 1 lemon (about 3 tablespoons)
½ medium-size purple onion, diced (about 1 cup)	2 tablespoons extra-virgin olive oil
½ English cucumber, diced (about ½ cup)	1 tablespoon capers
8 mint leaves, finely chopped	1 tablespoon champagne vinegar
2 tablespoons chopped flat-leaf parsley	½ teaspoon coarsely ground black pepper
	½ teaspoon salt

COMBINE all ingredients in a medium bowl. Stir mixture until well blended. Let stand at least 1 hour before serving. **Yield:** 5½ cups.

Tomato Tips

*Y*ou can find tomatoes in the marketplace year-round, but tomato season is really midsummer until the first frost. Tomato varieties vary in sweetness and acidity. From the tangy, under-ripe green tomato to the sweet orange tomato and from the juicy, bright red ripe tomato to the thick-skinned, meatier Roma, tomatoes are succulent and flavorful.

No matter the variety, select firm, brightly colored tomatoes that are heavy for their size. One of the best signs of ripeness is fragrance.

Store underripe to firm, ripe tomatoes at room temperature and away from direct sunlight. Only overripe tomatoes should be refrigerated. To enjoy maximum fresh flavor, plan to eat homegrown tomatoes the day you pick them.

FRESH VEGETABLE PICALILLI

4	cups fresh broccoli flowerets	1	cup rice vinegar
2	cups fresh cauliflower flowerets	1	cup tarragon vinegar
		1	cup white vinegar
2	large carrots, scraped and cut into ½-inch slices	½	cup sugar
		½	teaspoon salt
1	cucumber, peeled, halved lengthwise, seeded, and cut into 1-inch slices	¼	teaspoon celery seeds
		¼	teaspoon turmeric
		⅛	teaspoon dry mustard
1	large red bell pepper, cut into thin strips	⅛	teaspoon saffron threads (optional)

COMBINE first 5 ingredients in a large heavy-duty, zip-top plastic bag. Combine rice vinegar, next 7 ingredients, and saffron, if desired, in a saucepan; bring to a boil, stirring until sugar dissolves. Cool vinegar mixture slightly; pour vinegar mixture over broccoli mixture. Seal bag; chill 8 hours. Serve with a slotted spoon. **Yield:** 8 cups.

CHEDDAR-STUFFED APPLES

¼	cup chopped onion	1	large egg, lightly beaten
1	tablespoon butter or margarine, melted	¼	teaspoon salt
		¼	teaspoon apple pie spice
2	cups cubed cinnamon-raisin bread, toasted	4	Gala or other baking apples, cored and cut in half crosswise
1¼	cups (5 ounces) shredded sharp Cheddar cheese, divided	1	cup apple cider

COOK onion in butter in a large skillet over medium-high heat, stirring constantly, until tender. Stir in bread cubes, 1 cup cheese, and next 3 ingredients.

SPOON stuffing mixture evenly onto apple halves. (Cut a larger cavity in apples, if necessary, to hold stuffing mixture in place.) Place apples in a 13- x 9- x 2-inch baking dish; pour cider into dish. Cover and bake at 375° for 28 minutes. Uncover and sprinkle remaining ¼ cup cheese over apples; bake 2 more minutes or until cheese melts. **Yield:** 8 servings.

Bistro: Chef's Choice
ARTICHOKES AU GRATIN

Serve this dish over strands of pasta to show off the artichokes in this rich sauce.

3 (14-ounce) cans artichoke hearts, halved

4 cups heavy whipping cream

1 tablespoon butter

1 tablespoon finely chopped shallot

1 large clove garlic, minced

1 (8-ounce) package fresh mushrooms, sliced

2 tablespoons Biltmore Estate Chardonnay Sur Lies or other dry white wine

2 cups (8 ounces) shredded Monterey Jack cheese

1 cup freshly grated Parmesan cheese

½ teaspoon salt

¼ teaspoon ground white pepper

1 tablespoon chopped fresh basil

1 tablespoon chopped fresh oregano

2 tablespoons chopped fresh parsley

DRAIN artichokes, reserving liquid; set aside. Pour cream into a medium-size, heavy saucepan; bring to a simmer. Cook 15 minutes or until cream reduces to 2 cups; set aside.

HEAT butter in a large skillet over medium-high heat. Add shallot, garlic, and mushrooms; sauté 5 minutes. Stir in wine. Add reserved artichokes and half of reserved liquid; discard remaining liquid. Simmer 5 minutes or until almost dry. Stir in reserved cream; simmer 10 minutes. Gradually stir in cheeses until melted. Stir in salt, pepper, and remaining ingredients. Serve immediately over pasta, if desired. **Yield:** 8 servings.

CORN PUDDING

2 large eggs

½ cup whipping cream

1 tablespoon butter or margarine, melted

1½ teaspoons sugar

¼ teaspoon salt

¼ teaspoon pepper

3 cups fresh corn kernels

STIR together first 6 ingredients until well blended. Stir in corn kernels. Pour into a lightly greased 1½-quart baking dish. Bake at 350° for 30 minutes or until pudding is set. Let stand 5 minutes. **Yield:** 4 servings.

The Arresting Artichoke

The artichoke is a member of the thistle group of the sunflower family; the globe artichoke is most common (see photo). Artichokes are available fresh (whole), canned (hearts, quarters, and bottoms), or frozen (quarters). They add an extra dimension of flavor and interest to a variety of dishes.

Caramelized Onion Tart

GREEN BEAN AND FETA SAUTÉ

The sharp, salty flavor of feta cheese enlivens beans
and peppers without adding salt.

1	tablespoon olive oil	½	cup drained canned quartered artichoke hearts
½	pound fresh green beans, cut into 1-inch pieces	¼	cup canned vegetable broth or water
½	cup chopped onion	2	teaspoons lemon juice
½	cup red bell pepper strips Dash of dried crushed red pepper	2	tablespoons finely crumbled feta cheese

HEAT oil in a large nonstick skillet over medium-high heat until hot. Add green beans, onion, bell pepper, and crushed red pepper; sauté 3 minutes.

ADD artichokes and broth; cook until liquid is reduced to 2 tablespoons (about 30 seconds). Stir in lemon juice; sprinkle with cheese. **Yield:** 2 servings.

CARAMELIZED ONION TART

Natural sugar from onions is extracted over the initial lengthy cooking time,
providing sweet, caramelized flavor for this tart.

3	pounds large sweet onions, sliced	½	cup shredded Parmesan cheese
2	tablespoons olive oil		Garnish: fresh rosemary sprigs
1	teaspoon salt		
½	(17¼-ounce) package frozen puff pastry, thawed		

COOK onion in hot oil in a very large skillet or Dutch oven over low heat, stirring often, 30 to 35 minutes or until onion is caramel colored. Stir in salt, and set mixture aside.

UNFOLD pastry sheet; fit into a 9-inch square tart pan.

BAKE pastry at 400° for 15 to 20 minutes or until browned. Remove from oven. Press pastry with the back of a spoon to flatten. Top with caramelized onion; sprinkle with Parmesan cheese. Bake 5 more minutes. Garnish, if desired. **Yield:** 6 servings.

GINGERED PEARS IN ACORN SQUASH

To remove their skins, cook hazelnuts with 1 teaspoon baking soda in boiling water 30 to 45 seconds. Drain nuts; rub with towel (skins come off easily). Dry nuts before toasting.

3	medium acorn squash	1/3	cup butter or margarine, melted
2	ripe red pears, chopped (about 3 cups)	1	teaspoon Frangelico or other hazelnut-flavored liqueur (optional)
1/2	cup firmly packed brown sugar		
2	teaspoons minced peeled fresh ginger	1/2	cup chopped toasted hazelnuts

MAKE a small cut into each squash; microwave at HIGH 1 to 2 minutes to ease halving squash. Cut squash in half crosswise; remove and discard seeds. Place squash, cut side up, in a 13- x 9- x 2-inch baking dish.

COMBINE pear, brown sugar, ginger, butter, and, if desired, liqueur; spoon evenly into squash halves. Add boiling water to a depth of 1/2 inch to dish. Cover and bake at 350° for 1 hour and 15 minutes or until squash is tender. Transfer squash to a serving dish; sprinkle with toasted hazelnuts. **Yield:** 6 servings.

SUGAR SNAP PEAS WITH PAPAYA SALSA

The peppery spice of cilantro enhances the sweet aroma of the papaya in this versatile salsa. For a twist, serve it over fish.

1	cup diced fresh papaya	1/8	teaspoon salt
1/2	cup chopped fresh cilantro	1/8	teaspoon ground white pepper
1	tablespoon minced fresh onion	1	pound fresh sugar snap peas, trimmed
2	teaspoons lime juice		
2	teaspoons rice wine vinegar		

COMBINE first 7 ingredients in a small bowl; toss gently, and set aside.

ARRANGE sugar snap peas in a vegetable steamer over boiling water. Cover and steam 3 minutes or until peas are crisp-tender, and drain well. Transfer sugar snap peas to a serving bowl. Spoon salsa over sugar snap peas in bowl. Serve immediately. **Yield:** 4 servings.

Sugar Snap Peas with
Papaya Salsa

Meaty Portobellos

*T*he portobello—a fully mature common mushroom—is known for its large cap and prized for its meaty texture. Reduced moisture gives the portobello an earthy, concentrated flavor, making it the perfect complement to an entrée or served as a meatless entrée by itself.

Deerpark: Chef's Choice
PORTOBELLO MUSHROOMS WITH CABERNET SAUCE

The earthy flavors of the mushrooms and wine in the sauce also pair nicely with a tender filet mignon.

1 tablespoon olive oil	1 bay leaf
2 tablespoons diced shallot	4 sprigs fresh parsley, chopped
4 cloves garlic, minced	1 (14½-ounce) can beef broth
1 cup quartered fresh mushrooms	1 tablespoon all-purpose flour
¼ cup port wine	2 tablespoons port wine
¾ cup Biltmore Estate Cabernet Sauvignon or other dry red wine	½ teaspoon salt, divided
	¼ teaspoon freshly ground pepper
1 teaspoon chopped fresh thyme leaves	4 large portobello mushroom caps
	¼ cup olive oil

HEAT 1 tablespoon oil in a large skillet over medium-high heat. Add shallot, garlic, and mushrooms; sauté 3 minutes or until lightly browned. Add port; simmer 3 minutes or until liquid is absorbed. Add Cabernet Sauvignon, thyme, bay leaf, and parsley. Simmer 7 minutes or until reduced by one-half. Add beef broth; simmer 10 minutes or until reduced by one-forth. Discard bay leaf.

COMBINE flour and 2 tablespoons port in a small bowl, stirring until smooth. Add to wine mixture and simmer 3 minutes or until thickened. Add ¼ teaspoon salt and pepper. Set aside; keep warm.

REMOVE brown gills from the underside of portobello mushroom caps; slice caps.

HEAT ¼ cup oil in a large skillet over medium-high heat. Add sliced portobello caps and remaining ¼ teaspoon salt. Sauté 5 minutes or until golden, stirring often. Serve with warm sauce. **Yield:** 4 servings.

Winemaker's Notes: *Serve with Biltmore Estate Cabernet Sauvignon*

GARLIC NEW POTATOES

18 new potatoes, quartered
    (about 2¾ pounds)
¼ cup butter or margarine
2 cloves garlic, minced

1 tablespoon chopped fresh
   parsley
¼ teaspoon pepper

PLACE potato quarters in a saucepan; cover with salted water. Boil, covered, 10 minutes or until tender; drain.

MELT butter in a small skillet over medium-high heat; add garlic, and cook, stirring constantly, 3 minutes or until tender. Add parsley and pepper; pour over potato, tossing gently to coat. **Yield:** 6 servings.

APRICOT-GLAZED SWEET POTATOES

Fork-tender slices of sweet potato glisten with a glaze of apricot nectar, brown sugar, and butter. A generous topping of crunchy pecans adds toasty taste and texture appeal.

3 pounds medium-size sweet
   potatoes
1 cup firmly packed brown
   sugar
1½ tablespoons cornstarch
1 cup apricot nectar

2 tablespoons hot water
¼ teaspoon salt
⅛ teaspoon ground cinnamon
½ cup chopped pecans
2 tablespoons butter

PLACE potatoes in a saucepan; cover with water. Boil 10 minutes (potatoes will not be done). Cool to touch; peel potatoes, and cut into ½-inch-thick slices. Arrange potato slices in a lightly greased 2-quart casserole.

COMBINE brown sugar and next 5 ingredients in a small saucepan, stirring with a wire whisk. Cook, uncovered, over medium heat until thickened and bubbly, stirring often. Stir in pecans and butter. Pour sauce over potato slices. Bake, uncovered, at 350° for 45 minutes or until potato is tender. **Yield:** 6 servings.

ROASTED WINTER VEGETABLES

Warm up a cold weather meal with a wholesome vegetable side dish of hearty winter offerings such as turnips, parsnips, and butternut squash.

4 parsnips	¼ cup all-purpose flour
4 turnips	1 teaspoon freshly ground pepper
½ medium rutabaga	⅓ cup butter or margarine, melted
½ medium butternut squash	
2 quarts water	
2 tablespoons kosher salt, divided	

PEEL first 4 ingredients. Cut parsnips into 1-inch slices; cut turnips, rutabaga, and squash into 1-inch cubes.

BRING parsnip, turnip, rutabaga, 2 quarts water, and 1 tablespoon salt to a boil in a Dutch oven; boil 5 minutes, stirring occasionally. Add squash, and cook 7 to 10 minutes or until slightly tender. Drain and cool. Cover and chill up to 8 hours, if desired.

COMBINE remaining 1 tablespoon salt, flour, and pepper in a heavy-duty, zip-top plastic bag; add one-third of vegetables to bag. Seal and shake until coated; place vegetables in a single layer in a large greased roasting pan.

REPEAT procedure with remaining vegetables and flour mixture. Drizzle vegetables with butter, tossing gently to coat.

BAKE at 375° for 30 minutes or until golden. Serve immediately. **Yield:** 8 servings.

DESSERTS

Strawberry-Almond Romanoff,
page 149

HOLIDAY AMBROSIA

2 tablespoons flaked coconut
4 bananas, sliced
¼ cup orange juice
2 cups orange sections
1 cup fresh strawberries, halved

¼ cup salad dressing or
    mayonnaise
1 tablespoon sugar
½ cup whipping cream,
    whipped

SPREAD flaked coconut on an ungreased baking sheet. Bake at 350° for 3 to 5 minutes or until toasted, stirring often.

TOSS banana slices in orange juice; drain and reserve juice. Layer orange sections, banana slices, and strawberries in a serving bowl; cover and chill.

COMBINE salad dressing, sugar, and reserved orange juice; fold in whipped cream. Spoon over fruit; sprinkle with toasted coconut. **Yield:** 6 to 8 servings.

Deerpark: Chef's Choice
CHILLED APPLE SOUP

4 medium apples, quartered
    (about 1¼ pounds)
¼ cup sugar
1 (3-inch) cinnamon stick
1 (1-inch) slice fresh ginger
¾ cup Biltmore Estate Riesling
    or other sweet white wine

¼ cup apple juice
¼ cup beef broth
¼ cup sour cream
¼ cup whipping cream
½ teaspoon lemon juice

COMBINE first 6 ingredients in a saucepan. Bring to a boil; reduce heat, and simmer, covered, 45 minutes or until apples are tender. Remove apples from cooking liquid, reserving liquid; discard cinnamon and ginger.

REMOVE skins from apple wedges by holding edge of skin down with a fork and scooping pulp away from skin with a spoon. Discard skins. Return apple pulp to cooking liquid.

PROCESS apple mixture in a food processor until smooth. Combine apple puree, beef broth, and remaining ingredients in a medium bowl; stir until well blended. Cover and chill. **Yield:** 4 servings.

Winemaker's Notes: Serve with Biltmore Estate Riesling

PUMPKIN BREAD PUDDING

6 cups French bread cubes,
  toasted
2 cups half-and-half
3 large eggs, lightly beaten
1½ cups sugar
1 (15-ounce) can pumpkin
½ cup raisins

½ cup chopped pecans, toasted
3 tablespoons butter or
  margarine, melted
2 teaspoons pumpkin pie spice
1 teaspoon grated orange rind
  Whipped cream (optional)

PLACE bread cubes in a lightly greased 11- x 7- x 1½-inch baking dish.
Pour half-and-half over bread cubes.

STIR together eggs and next 7 ingredients, and gently fold into bread
cube mixture.

BAKE at 350° for 50 to 60 minutes or until set. Serve with whipped
cream, if desired. **Yield:** 8 servings.

STRAWBERRY-ALMOND ROMANOFF

*Named in honor of the Russian royal family, this deceptively simple dessert infuses
strawberries with almond liqueur. Serve the berries in parfait glasses for a
striking presentation as shown on page 147.*

1 quart fresh strawberries,
  halved
½ cup sugar
½ cup amaretto or other
  almond-flavored liqueur

1 cup whipping cream
2 tablespoons powdered sugar
1 teaspoon almond extract
  Garnishes: toasted almond
  slices, fresh mint sprigs

STIR together first 3 ingredients. Cover and chill 3 hours.

BEAT whipping cream at medium speed with an electric mixer until
foamy; gradually add powdered sugar and almond extract, beating until soft
peaks form.

SPOON strawberry halves into stemmed glasses, and top with sweetened
whipped cream. Garnish, if desired. **Yield:** 4 servings.

COMPANY COCONUT CAKE

To save time, substitute a package of white cake mix with
pudding, prepared and baked according to package directions, for the
homemade layers. But don't skimp on the frosting—canned could never
measure up to this rich, buttery version.

1 cup shortening	1 cup milk
2 cups sugar	1 teaspoon almond extract
4 large eggs	1 teaspoon vanilla extract
3 cups sifted cake flour	Coconut-Cream Cheese
2½ teaspoons baking powder	Frosting
½ teaspoon salt	

BEAT shortening at medium speed with an electric mixer until fluffy; gradually add sugar, beating well. Add eggs, one at a time, beating just until yellow disappears.

COMBINE flour, baking powder, and salt; add to shortening mixture alternately with milk, beginning and ending with flour mixture. Mix at low speed after each addition until blended. Stir in flavorings.

POUR batter into three greased and floured 9-inch round cakepans. Bake at 375° for 20 to 25 minutes or until a wooden pick inserted in center comes out clean. Cool in pans on wire racks 10 minutes; remove from pans, and cool completely on wire racks.

SPREAD Coconut-Cream Cheese Frosting between layers and on top and sides of cake. Store in refrigerator in an airtight container. **Yield:** one 3-layer cake.

COCONUT-CREAM CHEESE FROSTING

1 (8-ounce) package cream cheese, softened	1 teaspoon vanilla extract
½ cup butter or margarine, softened	1 (16-ounce) package powdered sugar, sifted
	1 (7-ounce) can flaked coconut

BEAT cream cheese and butter at medium speed with an electric mixer until creamy; add vanilla, beating well. Gradually add sugar, beating until smooth. Stir in coconut. **Yield:** 4 cups.

PEACH BRANDY POUND CAKE

*Need a quick-fix dessert? Keep a pound cake (or half a pound cake)
in your freezer; just slice it, and toast or grill the slices. Then top
with sliced fresh fruit, whipped cream, or ice cream.*

1 cup butter or margarine, softened	1 (8-ounce) carton sour cream
3 cups sugar	½ cup peach brandy
6 large eggs	2 teaspoons rum
3 cups all-purpose flour	1 teaspoon orange extract
¼ teaspoon baking soda	1 teaspoon vanilla extract
⅛ teaspoon salt	½ teaspoon lemon extract
	¼ teaspoon almond extract

BEAT butter at medium speed with an electric mixer 2 minutes or until
creamy. Gradually add sugar, beating 5 minutes. Add eggs, one at a time,
beating just until yellow disappears.

COMBINE flour, soda, and salt; add to butter mixture alternately with
sour cream, beginning and ending with flour mixture. Beat at low speed just
until blended after each addition. Stir in brandy and remaining ingredients.
Spoon batter into a greased and floured 10-inch tube pan.

BAKE at 325° for 1½ hours or until a wooden pick inserted in center
comes out clean. Cool in pan on a wire rack 10 to 15 minutes; remove from
pan, and cool completely on wire rack. **Yield:** one 10-inch cake.

Pondering the Pound Cake

*P*ound cakes get their name
from their original recipe—a
pound each of butter, sugar, flour,
and eggs. Today's pound cakes
have lightened up a bit by weight,
but still maintain that rich flavor
and tender crumb.

To ensure the best-textured
pound cake, always measure
ingredients precisely and mix the
batter properly. A critical step is
beating the butter or shortening
and sugar until light and fluffy
(see photo below). This procedure
takes about 5 minutes using an
electric mixer and ingredients that
have been at room temperature for
20 minutes. When adding eggs,
flour, and liquid to a recipe, mix
just until blended. Overbeating
can result in a tough cake.

TOFFEE MERINGUE TORTE

Two free-form meringues provide light and crispy layers for the
toffee bar "frosting." Warm toffee sauce caps the wedges nicely.

6 egg whites
¾ teaspoon cream of tartar
1 cup superfine sugar
8 (1.4-ounce) English toffee-
   flavored candy bars, frozen
   and crushed

2½ cups whipping cream,
    whipped
Toffee Sauce

LINE 2 baking sheets with parchment paper. Trace a 9-inch circle on
each, using a 9-inch round cakepan as a guide. Turn paper over; set aside.

BEAT egg whites at high speed with an electric mixer until foamy; add
cream of tartar, beating until soft peaks form. Add sugar, 2 tablespoons at a
time, beating until stiff peaks form. Spoon meringue mixture evenly inside
circles on baking sheets. Form each into a smooth circle.

BAKE at 275° for 2 hours. Turn oven off; cool slightly. Remove from
oven; peel off paper. Dry meringues on wire racks, away from drafts.

RESERVE 2 tablespoons crushed candy for garnish. Fold remaining
crushed candy into whipped cream. Chill or freeze until firm, but spreadable.

SPREAD whipped cream mixture between layers of meringue and on top
and sides of torte. Garnish with reserved candy. Plate torte in an airtight
cake cover; freeze at least 8 hours. Cut into wedges; serve with Toffee Sauce.
Yield: 8 to 10 servings.

TOFFEE SAUCE

1½ cups firmly packed brown
    sugar
½ cup light corn syrup

⅓ cup butter
⅔ cup whipping cream
1 teaspoon butter flavoring

COMBINE first 3 ingredients in a saucepan. Cook over medium heat
until mixture comes to a boil, stirring frequently. Remove from heat, and
cool 5 minutes. Stir in whipping cream and flavoring. Serve warm sauce with
torte. **Yield:** 2 cups.

WHITE CHOCOLATE-BROWNIE CHEESECAKE

Chunks of fudgy brownie in each slice enhance every sweet bite.

1½ cups graham cracker crumbs

2 tablespoons sugar

⅓ cup unsalted butter, melted

10 ounces white chocolate, broken into pieces

4 (8-ounce) packages cream cheese, softened

½ cup unsalted butter, softened

½ cup sugar

3 tablespoons all-purpose flour

4 large eggs

1½ tablespoons vanilla extract

Pinch of salt

2 cups coarsely chopped unfrosted brownies*

1 (16-ounce) carton sour cream

¼ cup sugar

½ teaspoon vanilla extract

COMBINE cracker crumbs, 2 tablespoons sugar, and ⅓ cup melted butter in a medium bowl, stirring well. Press mixture firmly in bottom and ½ inch up sides of a 10-inch springform pan. Chill 1 hour.

PLACE white chocolate pieces in top of a double boiler; bring water to a boil. Reduce heat to low; cook until chocolate melts, stirring frequently. Remove from heat, and stir until chocolate is smooth. Set aside, and let cool.

BEAT cream cheese and ½ cup butter at medium speed with an electric mixer 2 minutes or until light and fluffy. Combine ½ cup sugar and flour, stirring well; add to cream cheese mixture, beating well. Add eggs, one at a time, beating well after each addition. Add cooled chocolate, 1½ table-spoons vanilla, and salt; beat until well blended. Pour half of mixture into prepared crust. Top with chopped brownies; pour in remaining batter. Bake at 300° for 1 hour and 5 minutes.

COMBINE sour cream, ¼ cup sugar, and ½ teaspoon vanilla in a small bowl; stir well. Carefully spread sour cream mixture over cheesecake; bake 10 more minutes. Turn oven off, and leave cheesecake in oven with door open 1 hour. Remove from oven, and cool completely on a wire rack. Cover and chill 8 hours. Remove sides of pan before serving. **Yield:** 12 servings.

*Buy prepackaged unfrosted brownies from a bakery, or prepare your favorite mix; let cool and chop enough to yield 2 cups.

Blueberries and Cream Cheesecake

BLUEBERRIES AND CREAM CHEESECAKE

Cheesecake novices need not be intimidated. The rich sour cream topping and fresh blueberry glaze hide any flaws in the cheesecake.

1½ cups graham cracker crumbs

1½ cups plus 2 tablespoons sugar, divided

⅓ cup butter or margarine, melted

3½ cups fresh blueberries, divided

3 tablespoons cornstarch, divided

3 (8-ounce) packages cream cheese, softened

4 large eggs

¼ teaspoon salt

2 (8-ounce) cartons sour cream

½ teaspoon vanilla extract

¼ cup water

STIR together graham cracker crumbs, ¼ cup sugar, and butter. Press mixture evenly in bottom and ½ inch up sides of a 9-inch springform pan. Bake at 325° for 9 minutes. Cool.

PROCESS 2½ cups blueberries and 1 tablespoon cornstarch in container of an electric blender until smooth, stopping once to scrape down sides. Pour into a saucepan. Cook over medium heat, stirring constantly, about 15 minutes or until slightly thickened. Set mixture aside to cool. Cover and chill ½ cup mixture for making glaze.

BEAT cream cheese at medium speed with an electric mixer until light and fluffy. Gradually add 1 cup sugar, mixing well. Add eggs, 1 at a time, beating after each addition. Stir in remaining 2 tablespoons cornstarch and salt. Pour batter into prepared pan. Pour blueberry mixture over batter; gently swirl with a knife. Bake at 325° for 45 minutes or until set. Remove from oven; cool on a wire rack 20 minutes.

STIR together sour cream, 2 tablespoons sugar, and vanilla; spread over cheesecake. Bake at 325° for 10 more minutes. Cool in pan on wire rack. Cover and chill 8 hours.

STIR together reserved ½ cup blueberry mixture, remaining ¼ cup sugar, and ¼ cup water in a small saucepan; cook over medium heat, stirring constantly, until thickened. Gently fold in remaining 1 cup blueberries; cool. Remove sides of springform pan. Spoon blueberry glaze over cheesecake. **Yield:** 10 to 12 servings.

BLACK BOTTOM PEANUT BUTTER PIE

Our chefs pipe decorative mounds of whipped cream to top this lush pie, but swirling the cream on top works just as well. If you choose to pipe it, chill the pastry bag and its tip first. This keeps the heat of your hand from melting the whipped cream.

3 (1-ounce) squares semisweet chocolate	2 (8-ounce) packages cream cheese, softened
1½ tablespoons butter, softened	1⅓ cups sugar
2 tablespoons whipping cream Cream-Filled Chocolate Sandwich Cookie Pastry Shell	1 cup creamy peanut butter
	¾ cup whipping cream
	2 tablespoons sifted powdered sugar

COMBINE first 3 ingredients in a heavy saucepan; cook over low heat until blended and smooth, stirring often. Spread chocolate mixture in bottom of pastry shell; let cool 5 minutes. Cover and chill 30 minutes.

BEAT cream cheese at medium speed with an electric mixer until light and fluffy. Add sugar and peanut butter, beating well. Spoon filling over chocolate mixture in pastry shell; smooth with a spatula.

BEAT whipping cream at medium speed with an electric mixer until foamy; gradually add powdered sugar, beating until soft peaks form. Spoon sweetened whipped cream into a pastry bag; pipe cream onto pie using a large star tip. Freeze until firm. Let stand 10 minutes at room temperature before serving. **Yield:** one 9-inch pie.

CREAM-FILLED CHOCOLATE SANDWICH COOKIE PASTRY SHELL

Use an electric blender or food processor to produce smooth crumbs.

2 cups cream-filled chocolate sandwich cookie crumbs (about 20 cookies)	2 tablespoons butter, melted

COMBINE crumbs and melted butter in a medium bowl. Firmly press mixture evenly in bottom and up sides of a well-greased 9-inch pieplate. **Yield:** one 9-inch pastry shell.

SWEET POTATO PIE WITH STREUSEL TOPPING

Streusel is the German word for sprinkle. The crunchy, nutty topping makes this dessert a holiday favorite.

5 ounces cream cheese (about ⅔ cup)	¾ cup sugar
1 large egg	½ teaspoon salt
¼ cup sugar	½ teaspoon ground cinnamon
1 baked 9-inch pastry shell	½ teaspoon ground ginger
2 large eggs, lightly beaten	⅛ teaspoon ground nutmeg
4 cooked small sweet potatoes, mashed (about 1½ cups)	½ cup half-and-half
	Streusel Topping

BEAT cream cheese, 1 egg, and ¼ cup sugar at medium speed with an electric mixer until creamy. Spread mixture into baked pastry shell.

COMBINE beaten eggs and mashed sweet potato. Add ¾ cup sugar and next 4 ingredients; stir in half-and-half. Pour sweet potato mixture over cream cheese layer.

BAKE at 350° for 25 minutes. Sprinkle Streusel Topping over pie; bake 25 to 30 more minutes or until topping is golden. **Yield:** one 9-inch pie.

STREUSEL TOPPING

½ cup quick-cooking oats	2 tablespoons sugar
⅓ cup chopped pecans	½ teaspoon ground cinnamon
¼ cup all-purpose flour	¼ cup butter, melted

COMBINE first 5 ingredients; stir well. Add butter, and stir until crumbly. **Yield:** 1⅓ cups.

Winemaker's Notes: *Serve with Biltmore Estate Special Reserve Chenin Blanc*

Raspberry Rhapsody

*A*vailable from May to November, the raspberry is one of a few fruits that tempts you with both its sweetness and tartness. Raspberries are really several individual fruit sections joined by a core. Although the red variety usually comes to mind, raspberries also produce golden and black fruits.

Select plump berries that aren't shriveled, soft, or moldy, and store them in a single layer, if possible, sealed in a moisture-proof container in the refrigerator.

RASPBERRY CREAM PIE

1 cup sugar	⅓ cup all-purpose flour
⅓ cup all-purpose flour	⅓ cup firmly packed brown
2 large eggs, lightly beaten	sugar
1⅓ cups sour cream	⅓ cup chopped pecans
1 teaspoon vanilla extract	3 tablespoons butter, softened
3 cups fresh raspberries*	Garnishes: whipped cream,
1 unbaked 9-inch pastry shell	fresh raspberries

COMBINE first 5 ingredients in a large bowl, stirring until smooth. Gradually fold in raspberries. Spoon into pastry shell. Bake at 400° for 30 to 35 minutes or until a knife inserted in center comes out clean.

COMBINE ⅓ cup flour and next 3 ingredients; sprinkle over hot pie. Bake at 400° for 10 more minutes or until golden. Garnish, if desired. **Yield:** one 9-inch pie.

*Do not substitute frozen raspberries for fresh in this pie.

Stable Café: Chef's Choice
NORTH CAROLINA APPLE AND HAZELNUT TART

1 cup plus 1 tablespoon all-purpose flour, divided	¼ cup sugar
	1 large egg, lightly beaten
⅓ cup sugar	1 tablespoon Frangelico or
½ cup chopped hazelnuts, divided	other hazelnut-flavored
	liqueur
¼ teaspoon vanilla extract	1 tablespoon sugar
½ cup butter	½ teaspoon ground cinnamon
1 (8-ounce) package cream cheese, softened	2 small cooking apples, peeled and thinly sliced

COMBINE 1 cup flour, ⅓ cup sugar, ¼ cup hazelnuts, and vanilla; cut in butter with a pastry blender or two knives until mixture is crumbly. Press mixture in bottom and up sides of a 9-inch tart pan. Bake at 350° for 15 minutes.

BEAT cream cheese and ¼ cup sugar at medium speed with an electric mixer until creamy. Add egg and liqueur; beat well. Pour into crust.

COMBINE remaining 1 tablespoon flour, 1 tablespoon sugar, and cinnamon in a medium bowl; add sliced apple to cinnamon mixture, and toss gently. Overlap slices in a circle over cream cheese mixture; sprinkle with remaining ¼ cup hazelnuts. Bake at 350° for 50 minutes or until cheese mixture is set. **Yield:** one 9-inch tart.

Winemaker's Notes: Serve with Biltmore Estate Riesling

Deerpark: Chef's Choice
LEMON TART

¼ cup butter, softened	1 cup fresh lemon juice
¼ cup sugar	⅓ cup heavy whipping cream
⅛ teaspoon salt	¼ cup plus 2 tablespoons
1 large egg	butter, cut into small
1½ cups all-purpose flour	pieces
1½ cups sugar	Garnishes: whipped cream,
1 tablespoon cornstarch	grated lemon rind
6 large eggs	

BEAT first 3 ingredients at medium speed with a heavy-duty mixer until combined. Add egg, beating well. Add flour; mix just until combined. Wrap in plastic wrap and flatten to a 6-inch disk. Chill 2 hours.

ROLL pastry to ⅛-inch thickness on a lightly floured surface. Place in a 9-inch tart pan; trim off excess pastry along edges. Line pastry with aluminum foil or wax paper; fill with pie weights or dried beans. Bake at 350° for 10 minutes. Remove foil, and bake 3 more minutes. Cool completely.

COMBINE 1½ cups sugar and cornstarch; stir well. Combine cornstarch mixture, 6 eggs, lemon juice, and cream in a heavy saucepan; stir well with a wire whisk. Add butter. Cook over medium-low heat, stirring constantly, until temperature reaches 160°, about 10 minutes. Reduce heat and simmer, uncovered, 3 minutes, stirring constantly.

POUR mixture into cooled tart shell. Bake at 350° for 20 minutes or until filling is set. Cool completely; cover and chill. Garnish, if desired. **Yield:** one 9-inch tart.

PEAR DUMPLINGS

Tender homemade pastry wraps up the taste of fall in these shapely dumplings.
We recommend using either Bosc or Bartlett pears, which hold up well
during the long cooking time.

3 cups all-purpose flour	½ cup chopped macadamia nuts
2 teaspoons baking powder	¼ cup cold butter or margarine, cut up
1 teaspoon salt	
1 cup shortening	1½ cups sugar
¾ cup milk	1½ cups water
6 medium-size firm, ripe pears, such as Bosc or Bartlett	1 tablespoon butter or margarine
	Rind of 1 medium-size orange, cut into strips
¼ cup firmly packed brown sugar	1 (3-inch) slice fresh ginger
1 teaspoon ground cinnamon	

COMBINE first 3 ingredients; cut in shortening with a pastry blender or two knives until mixture is crumbly. Gradually add milk, stirring to make a soft dough. Turn dough out onto a lightly floured surface, and roll into a 21- x 14-inch rectangle. Cut rectangle into 6 (7-inch) squares using a pastry wheel.

PEEL pears, reserving skin. Core each pear from bottom, leaving top 2 inches. Place each pear, bottom side down, on a pastry square.

STIR together brown sugar, cinnamon, and chopped nuts; spoon 2 teaspoonfuls mixture into each pear core, pressing firmly. Dot tops of pears evenly with ¼ cup butter.

MOISTEN pastry edges with water. Bring corners to center, pinching edges to seal. Place pear dumplings in a lightly greased 13- x 9- x 2-inch baking dish.

BAKE at 375° for 40 to 50 minutes, shielding with aluminum foil after 30 minutes to prevent excessive browning.

BRING reserved pear skin, 1½ cups sugar, and next 4 ingredients to a boil in a medium saucepan over medium-high heat. Reduce heat; simmer, stirring occasionally, 4 minutes or until butter melts and sugar dissolves. Remove from heat. Pour through a wire-mesh strainer into a bowl, discarding solids. Pour syrup over dumplings. Serve immediately. **Yield:** 6 servings.

Pear Dumplings

PÂTÉ À CHOUX WITH PASTRY CREAM

Better known as cream-puff pastry or choux pastry, the base for this dessert is simply butter, flour, and eggs stirred vigorously on the cooktop and then baked into delicate, airy pastries that puff. Space a few inches apart on the baking sheet to allow room to expand during cooking.

1 cup water	½ cup plus 2 tablespoons bread
¼ cup cold butter, cut up	flour
¼ teaspoon salt	5 large eggs
½ cup cake flour	Pastry Cream (page 19)

BRING first 3 ingredients to a boil in a medium saucepan over medium-high heat; reduce heat to low.

SIFT together flours. Stir into butter mixture, beating with a wooden spoon 1½ to 2 minutes or until mixture leaves sides of pan. Remove from heat; cool slightly.

BEAT eggs into flour mixture, one at a time, at medium speed with a heavy-duty mixer fitted with a paddle attachment, beating until smooth after each addition.

LINE a large baking sheet with parchment paper. Drop batter by heaping teaspoonfuls, 2 inches apart, onto baking sheets. Bake at 425° for 10 minutes. Reduce heat to 375°; bake 10 to 12 more minutes until golden. Transfer to a wire rack to cool.

CUT tops from Pâté à Choux; fill each pastry shell evenly with Pastry Cream. **Yield:** 30 Pâté à Choux.

Deerpark: Chef's Choice
CHOCOLATE TRUFFLES

1 pound semisweet chocolate, chopped

¾ cup heavy whipping cream

¼ cup bourbon, rum, Grand Marnier or other liqueur

Coatings: chopped toasted almonds, walnuts, or pecans; chocolate sprinkles; or cocoa

MELT chocolate in top of a double boiler over simmering water. Gradually stir in cream. Gradually add bourbon, stirring gently to blend. Cover and chill overnight.

SHAPE mixture into 1¾-inch balls, using 2 level tablespoons of mixture; roll in desired coatings. **Yield:** 16 truffles.

Winemaker's Notes: Serve with Château Biltmore Cabernet Sauvignon

GOLDEN ALMOND ICE CREAM BALLS

2 pints vanilla ice cream

2 (6-ounce) cans honey-roasted almonds

1 cup flaked coconut

½ cup honey

½ cup amaretto or other almond-flavored liqueur

SCOOP ice cream into 8 balls; freeze until firm.

PROCESS almonds and coconut in a food processor or an electric blender until finely chopped. Roll ice cream balls in almond mixture, and freeze until firm. Transfer ice cream balls to serving dishes.

COMBINE honey and amaretto; drizzle over ice cream balls just before serving. **Yield:** 8 servings.

Making Granitas and Sorbets

*W*hen making sorbets and granitas, keep the following tips in mind:

• To help develop the desired icy consistency, chill the ingredients before freezing.

• Cover sorbets and granitas while they freeze; otherwise, they may pick up flavors from other foods or excess moisture that can make them sticky.

• To achieve its characteristically granular texture, stir a granita several times while it freezes. Use a fork to scrape and shave the mixture until it's fluffy for serving (see photo below).

• For the smooth but icy consistency of sorbets, process the almost frozen mixture in a food processor just until fluffy. Freeze mixture again until firm.

• Sorbets left in the freezer more than a few days can become too crystallized. If this happens, partially thaw the sorbet, and process it again in the food processor. Refreeze and use it within 24 hours.

CAPPUCCINO GRANITA

This Sicilian classic starts with double-strength brewed coffee (dark roast is best) to heighten the coffee flavor when the mixture is frozen.

½ cup ground coffee beans
1¾ cups water
⅓ cup sugar
⅓ cup water
1 teaspoon vanilla extract
¼ teaspoon ground cinnamon
½ cup milk
Garnish: fresh mint sprigs

ASSEMBLE drip coffeemaker according to manufacturer's directions. Place ground coffee in the coffee filter or filter basket. Add 1¾ cups water to coffeemaker and brew; set coffee aside.

COMBINE sugar and ⅓ cup water in a small saucepan. Bring to a boil, and cook 1 minute or until sugar dissolves. Stir in vanilla and cinnamon. Remove from heat, and stir in brewed coffee and milk.

COOL coffee mixture completely; pour into an 8-inch square baking dish. Cover and freeze at least 8 hours or until firm. Remove coffee mixture from freezer; scrape entire mixture with a fork until fluffy. Spoon into a freezer-safe container; cover and freeze for up to 1 month. Garnish, if desired. **Yield:** 6 servings.

WATERMELON SORBET

Use summer's sweetest, freshest melon for this refreshing dessert.

4 cups water
2 cups sugar
8 cups chopped seeded watermelon
1 (12-ounce) can frozen pink lemonade concentrate, thawed and undiluted

BRING 4 cups water and sugar just to a boil in a medium saucepan over high heat, stirring until sugar dissolves. Remove from heat. Cool.

PROCESS sugar syrup and watermelon in batches in container of an electric blender until smooth. Stir in lemonade concentrate. Cover and chill 2 hours.

POUR mixture into freezer container of a 1-gallon electric freezer. Freeze according to manufacturer's instructions. **Yield:** 2½ quarts.

BILTMORE ESTATE WINES

Château Biltmore Collection

Château Biltmore Chardonnay

Fermented and aged in small, toasted oak barrels, this dry, crisp wine has a blend of lime, grapefruit, and pear aromas with a touch of vanilla.

Château Biltmore Claret

Distinctive Cabernet Sauvignon, Cabernet Franc, and Merlot combine to create a classic, velvety red wine. The fruity flavor hints of almond and vanilla.

Château Biltmore Cabernet Sauvignon

Dark cherry color, concentrated berry flavor, and a touch of oak highlight this exceptional wine.

Sparkling Wines

Château Biltmore Méthode Champenoise-Brut

Brilliant and luminous with tiny bubbles, this world-class wine offers autumnal aroma while honey, citrus, and mint flavors linger in its buttery finish. It's an outstanding dinner wine bringing perfection to every meal.

Blanc de Blanc-Brut

Rich golden color and fine bubbles complement the hint of hazelnut, strong fruit aroma, and neat acid of our award-winning "Méthode Champenoise" Brut.

Blanc de Blanc-Sec

We produce our Sec Sparkling Wine in the traditional "Méthode Champenoise"—fermenting each bottle individually. Serve this sweeter selection on special occasions, or with brunch, cold foods, and desserts.

White Wines

Sauvignon Blanc

Aged for a few months in small oak barrels, our classic dry white wine exhibits floral and exotic fruit aromas with a hint of vanilla. Pair with fish, shrimp, and shellfish.

Chardonnay Sur Lies

This dry Chardonnay is aged in its sediment during fall and winter, adding a subtle fruit aroma and a pleasant, complex character. Enjoy with salads, light dishes, and seafood.

Chardonnay #21 (Semi-Sweet)

Delicately sweet, this popular varietal is ideal with poultry and pasta. Serve chilled.

American Riesling

A very floral, spicy aroma and a crisp, spicy flavor combine in this appealing white wine. Pair with cold vegetable soups, fruit tarts, and pastries as well as sweet and sour dishes, or serve as an apéritif.

Chenin Blanc

Made with the legendary Chenin Blanc grape, this full-bodied, fruity wine is accentuated by a sweet finish and complements a variety of desserts. Serve well-chilled.

Special Reserve Chenin Blanc

One of our sweetest selections, Special Reserve begins with very ripe grapes. A golden color and a tropical bouquet enrich this ideal dessert wine noted for its wonderful balance and lingering finish.

Rosé Wines

Zinfandel Blanc de Noir

This complex wine with hints of cherry, lemon, and raspberry aromas pairs perfectly with spicy and grilled foods. It's a perfect addition to summer cookouts and picnics.

Cabernet Blanc de Noir

The delicate floral aroma and refreshing fruity flavor of this semisweet rosé go well with Asian cuisine. Serve well-chilled.

Red Wines

Cabernet Sauvignon

Deep cherry red color, complex aroma, and hints of spices and smooth tannins define this rich, elegant wine. Serve at room temperature to complement a variety of meats.

Cardinal's Crest®

Serve this dry, full-bodied, velvety wine with lamb, white meats, and fish.

Merlot

Soft, with elegant undertones of spices and plum, our inherently complex Merlot complements poultry and red meats.

Cerise

Smoky aromas of cherry, raspberry, and leather lead to a distinctive peppery finish, making this an excellent companion to Italian pasta and spicy foods.

Cabernet Franc

This dry, oak-aged red wine is medium in body and delightfully smooth. It is an excellent accompaniment to lamb, beef, or pork.

WINE APPRECIATION

When the Vanderbilts and their friends dined at the Biltmore House, the standard was haute cuisine and bottles of fine wine. Today, Biltmore Estate wines are created in the same spirit, only gourmet fare isn't a necessity. Our wines complement tables ranging from simple to ambitious. No matter the varietal you choose, our wines pair particularly well with good conversation.

And while there are acknowledged customs regarding the pairing of food and wine, there are no hard and fast rules. There are, however, several things to consider when pairing wines with food.

No matter the varietal you choose, our wines pair particularly well with good conversation.

FOOD & WINE PAIRING

Wines get their name either from the grape that was used to make them (Chardonnay, Merlot, Cabernet Sauvignon) or the region in which they were made (Burgundy, Chianti, Sauternes). Generally, wine and food from the same region can be a good pairing, like sausage with Riesling from Germany or pasta with Chianti from Italy. As wines become increasingly known by their grape variety rather than their region, you may want to experience a wine tasting or two to develop your own personal preferences.

The way a food is prepared is more important in determining the wine to be served than the food itself. For instance, try a light white wine such as Sauvignon Blanc with grilled chicken, but enjoy a full-bodied Chardonnay with chicken in cream sauce—and consider a rosé or red wine for chicken cooked with heavier Italian or Chinese flavors.

The simplest approach to food and wine pairing: When food and wines have similar flavors and characteristics, they won't overpower each other. This is why you might serve a sweet Sauternes with dessert. To match the tart flavors of feta and garlic in popular Mediterranean dishes, an acidic wine such as Chardonnay is a good choice.

You may prefer to choose a wine that contrasts with your food. Salty dishes like smoked salmon are enhanced served with a slightly sweet wine like a Riesling. Serve a light, acidic wine such as Sauvignon Blanc with a rich food like beef tenderloin with a cream sauce. Because alcohol accentuates heat, spicy foods also work well with slightly sweet wines because of their lower alcohol content.

WINE TASTING

Your sense of smell plays a major role in sampling and selecting wines. A wine's fragrance is called its nose or bouquet. The scents you detect depend on the type of grape used, where it was grown, if the wine was aged in oak barrels, and how long it has been in the bottle.

Wines reveal their best qualities when served

correctly. For example, wine must be served at optimum temperature, the cork extracted neatly, and the wine served in an appropriately shaped glass. Some pointers:

•**Temperature check:** Serve white wines just out of the refrigerator or slightly warmer; the sweeter the wine, the cooler the recommended serving temperature. Light, young red wines taste best between 55° and 60°; full-bodied reds are typically enjoyed at 60° to 65°. You can always start with wine a little too cold; it warms up quickly as a meal gets under way.

•**Serving savvy:** Wine should be opened gently, using an opener that enables you to extract the cork cleanly. Be sure to wipe off the rim of the bottle before serving the wine. If served from the bottle, twist the bottle as you pour to prevent dripping. Fill a wine glass only one-half to two-thirds full (one-third for a wine tasting). Fine table wines come in a 750-milliliter bottle; it is a little less than a quart, and contains five to six glasses of wine. A split is a 375-milliliter half-bottle, perfect for an intimate occasion.

•**Order, order:** If you're serving more than one wine with a meal, serve dry before sweet, white before red, light before full-bodied, and young before aged.

• **The tasting:** To swirl and taste wine, grasp the stem of the glass rather than the bowl to avoid raising the wine's temperature. Set the glass on the table and swirl it cautiously. Then bring the glass quickly to your nose, breathe deeply, and savor a sip. Sample a variety of wines to familiarize yourself with all types.

•**Wine glass class:** Red wine glasses have larger bowls than white wine glasses. This allows more room for swirling so that you can enjoy the big bouquet that is the trademark of fine red wine. Ideally, a wine glass should be thin, with the rim of the glass as thin as the glass itself.

•**Good to the last drop:** Recork leftover wine and refrigerate it up to two days.

In a Restaurant

In many restaurants, the waitstaff is coached on recommended wine pairings for specific menu items. Let them know your price range and what you are having for dinner. If you and your guests are eating different food, you can either compromise on a bottle of "all-purpose wine" such as a light red (not too sweet or too acidic) or order by the glass. A bottle is usually cheaper than buying by the glass.

When your server brings the bottle to your table, examine the label to verify it's what you ordered. If you are given the cork, make sure it isn't dried out or crumbly—a sign of improper storage or previous opening. Next, the server will pour a sip of wine. Swirl it around in the glass, smell it, and taste it. If it smells "off" or tastes vinegary, send it back—but don't return it just because you don't like it as much as you had hoped. After your approval, the waiter serves others at your table.

Taste & Aroma

*M*atch all three of these white wines with most poultry, fish, and shellfish recipes, particularly grilled.

• **Chardonnay** is perhaps the most popular of all white wine grapes. It's generally a deep golden color, which hints that it has been aged in oak barrels. Usually dry, Chardonnay has buttery, fruity, vanilla, and toasty flavors. It pairs well with a host of entrées.

• **Sauvignon Blanc** is a dry white wine that is lighter in color and body and more citrusy and herbaceous than Chardonnay. It is a food-friendly wine with an acidic zing.

• **Riesling** is a light, fruity wine with a floral fragrance.

*R*ed wines aren't just served with red meats anymore. Find your preference.

• **Cabernet Sauvignon** is a deep, rich, ruby-red wine with peppery, berry, and vanilla qualities from oak aging. "Cab" is a big, full-bodied, and intense wine. It pairs well with beef, poultry, pasta, and game meats.

• **Merlot** also has a deep ruby color and is a softer, more supple red wine than Cab. Its flavor can hint of berry, black cherry, plum, spice, and tobacco. It pairs well with poultry and lamb.

• **Pinot Noir** is more delicate than the two reds listed above. Hints of spicy cherries with earthy nuances create a complex flavor. It pairs well with beef and ham.

WINE & FOOD PAIRING CHART

FOOD	WINES *(Those listed by grape variety are in regular type; regional wines are in italic.)*
Hot, spicy foods *Ingredients like:* chiles, ginger, and pepper *Common cuisines:* Chinese, Indian, Mexican, and Thai	**Slightly sweet, fruity, light wines** such as *Burgundy,* Chenin Blanc, Gamay Beaujolais, Gewürztraminer, Pinot Noir, Riesling, *Rhone wines,* and light Zinfandels
Acidic, tart foods *Ingredients like:* feta cheese, garlic, lemon, tomatoes, vinegar, citrus *Common cuisines:* Creole, Greek, Italian, and Japanese	**High-acid wines** such as Chardonnay, *Chianti,* Sauvignon Blanc, and sparkling whites
Rich foods *Ingredients like:* butter, cheese, lobster, red meats, and salmon *Common cuisines:* French, German, Italian, and Southern	**Acidic, citrus wine** such as Sauvignon Blanc **Oaky, toasty, buttery wine** such as Chardonnay **Tannic (tart), darker reds** like Cabernet Sauvignon, Merlot, and dark Zinfandel
Salty or smoked foods *Ingredients like:* olives, salt-cured or smoked meats, and soy sauce *Common cuisines:* Japanese, German, Greek, and Southern	**Slightly sweet, fruity light wines** such as Chenin Blanc, Gamay Beaujolais, Gewürztraminer, Pinot Noir, Riesling, sparkling wine, and light Zinfandels
Sweet foods *Ingredients like:* coconut, corn, fruits, mint, and thyme *Common cuisines:* Chinese, French, Indian, and Thai	**For foods other than desserts: slightly sweet wines** such as Chenin Blanc, Riesling, and Gewürztraminer **For desserts: sweet wines** such as Madeira, Ruby Port, *Sauternes,* sherry, and sparkling wines such as Asti Spumante *Note:* Pair sweet foods with sweet wines, but the food should never be sweeter than the wine.

HERB DICTIONARY

*H*erbs are versatile, offering simple fresh seasoning to almost any type of food—even some desserts. Here are some simple tips for enjoying fresh herbs:

• If you grow your own herbs for cooking, use them before they flower. Harvest herbs early in the morning just after the dew has dried. Wash herbs and pat dry.

• If you buy fresh herbs at the grocery store, preserve them up to a week with one of the following methods:

1) Wrap stems in a soaking wet paper towel, taking care to keep herb foliage dry, and place in a zip-top plastic bag. Seal bag with air inside and store in refrigerator.

2) Place stem ends in a glass with two inches of water; cover foliage loosely with a plastic bag, and store in refrigerator.

• If a recipe doesn't specify when to add herbs, it's best to add them near the end of cooking to release their full flavor. Bay leaves are the exception; they typically simmer at length in soups.

• If you substitute fresh herbs for dried herbs (which are more concentrated in flavor), use three times the amount of fresh herbs as dried. Rosemary is the exception; use it in equal amounts.

• When blending herbs, choose a leading flavor and combine it with a more subtle, background herb. Don't emphasize more than one strong herb in a dish. **Strong herbs** are rosemary, cilantro, thyme, oregano, and sage; add sparingly because they contribute quite a bit of flavor to a dish. **Medium-flavored herbs** are basil, dill, mint, and fennel; use them more generously. Use **delicate herbs** like parsley and chives in abundance.

DICTIONARY

Following are a variety of herbs to introduce you to a world of fresh seasonings.

Basil: Easy to grow, basil is best in salads, pestos, pasta dishes, pizza, and meat and poultry dishes. Purple ruffles basil (shown) has curly purple-black leaves with a mild fragrance and flavor.

Bay Leaves: Use fresh or dried leaves in soups, vegetables, and bouquet garnis. Discard whole leaves before serving food.

Borage: The purple flowers of borage are popular edible garnishes in salads, on cakes, or floating in a glass of wine or tea. Young leaves can also be used but wilt quickly. Chop and add to salads or cucumber tea sandwiches just before serving.

Chervil: Commonly known as French parsley, it has a subtle anise flavor and is best fresh or cooked briefly. Add chervil to egg dishes, soups, or salads, or use it as a substitute for parsley.

Chives: Attractive and easy to grow, snipped chives provide a mild onion or garlic flavor to soups, salads, and vegetable dishes. In spring, chives boast globelike lavender-colored blooms that make ideal edible garnishes for salads. The wild (nodding) onion shown is a type of chive in bloom.

Cilantro/Coriander: Also known as Chinese parsley, spicy-flavored cilantro is the leaf; coriander is the seed or powder. The two are not interchangeable in recipes. Use the leaves in Southwestern, Mexican, and Asian dishes. Coriander seeds are used in Indian dishes as well as pickles and relishes.

Dill: A good salt substitute, finely chop feathery fresh dill foliage for shrimp dishes, eggs, soups, sandwiches, potato salad, and sauces.

Geranium, Scented: Both the foliage and flowers are edible. Use scented leaves for flavoring pound cakes, cookies, herb butters, jellies, and tea. Scented varieties include apple, lemon, orange, peppermint, rose (shown), and strawberry.

Lavender: Edible and ornamental, this herb has purple flowers that spike in early summer. Harvest the flowers just before fully opened for use in ice cream or other desserts, marinades, and sauces. Spanish lavender, shown, is a gray-leafed plant with needlelike leaves that resemble rosemary.

Lemon Balm: This hardy, bushy member of the mint family has a mild lemony flavor. Chop the aromatic leaves to use in tea bread, scones, and salads, or use whole leaves in tea or other cold beverages.

Lemon Verbena: The strongest scented lemon herb, use it as you would lemon balm leaves. Pulse a handful of leaves with a cup of sugar in a food processor to make lemon sugar. Store it in a jar, and use the sugar in desserts and teas.

Mint: Add this popular herb to lamb, poultry, salads, sauces, teas, and punches. Try cooking with flavorful varieties of mint like peppermint, orange mint, apple mint, or chocolate mint. Shown are the common spearmint and variegated pineapple mint.

Nasturtiums: These bright red and orange edible flowers (shown below) have a peppery taste. Use them in salads, sandwich spreads, or as a versatile garnish.

Oregano: Greek oregano is the most popular type for cooking because of its strong flavor and aromatic leaves. Add oregano to Italian dishes, meat, fish, eggs, fresh and cooked tomatoes, vegetables, beans, and marinades.

Rosemary: Unlike other herbs, fresh rosemary has a stronger flavor than its dried version. It's a hardy herb with a piney scent and flavor. To harvest rosemary, strip leaves from the stem. Use the strong-flavored leaves sparingly. Rosemary adds a wonderful accent to soups, meats, stews, breads, and vegetables.

Sage: This fuzzy, gray-green, hardy herb is best known as an ingredient in holiday dressings. Sage is also often paired with sausage. Its soft texture makes it easy to tuck under the skin of poultry before roasting.

Tarragon: Enjoy this tender herb in a classic béarnaise sauce. Tarragon also adds flavor to soups, poultry, seafood, vegetables, and egg dishes, and it is used often to make herb butter or vinegar. French tarragon is shown. Its leaves have a bittersweet, peppery scent with a hint of anise.

Thyme: Strip the tiny leaves from stems just before using. Use fresh thyme in marinades for basting seafood, chicken, or pork. Add thyme to mayonnaise for sandwiches or to beans, meat stews, vegetables, or rice. Among the many varieties of thyme is lime thyme, shown below.

RECIPE INDEX

SOURCES & ACKNOWLEDGEMENTS

Cover
gold cloth:
Ann Gish
3529 Old Conejo Road
Newbury Park, CA 91320
(805) 498-4447

Pages 2-3
pitcher:
Eigen Arts, Inc.
150 Bay Street
Jersey City, NJ 07302
(201) 798-7310

Pages 26-27
flatware:
Sabre
Paris, France

ramekins:
Williams Sonoma
(800) 541-2233

red and white bowl:
Ronnie's Ceramics Co.
5999 3rd Street
San Francisco, CA 94124
(415) 822-8068

Pages 32-33
container for bread:
Smith & Hawkin
(800) 776-5558

enamel plates and mugs:
McKenzie Childs
3260 State Route 90
Aurora, NY 13026-9769
(315) 364-7123

glasses:
Mariposa
5 Elm Street
Manchester, MA 01944
(978) 526-9944

Pages 44-45
pedestal and tray:
Terra Firma
152 West 25th Street
New York, NY 10001
(212) 645-7600

Pages 50-51
copper candlesticks and candles:
RAH
1413 23rd Street
Galveston, TX 77550
(409) 621-4652

copper samavar:
Bridges Antiques
3949 Cypress Drive
Cahaba Heights, AL 35243
(205) 967-6233

napkins:
Table Matters
2409 Montevallo Road
Mountain Brook, AL 35223
(205) 879-0125

Pages 56-57
china: (SASAKI Tartan)
Bromberg and Co.
2800 Cahaba Road
Mountain Brook, AL 35223
(205) 871-3276

tree candles:
Crate & Barrel
(800) 451-8217

utensils:
Mariposa
5 Elm Street
Manchester, MA 01944
(978) 526-9944

Pages 62-63
gratin dishes:
Williams Sonoma
(800) 541-2233

Pages 68-69
silver casserole holder and pitcher:
Bromberg and Co.
2800 Cahaba Road
Mountain Brook, AL 35223
(205) 871-3276

plaid red box:
Henhouse Antiques
1900 Cahaba Road
Birmingham, AL 35223
(205) 918-0505

Pages 74-75
table and chairs:
Village Antiques
755 Biltmore Avenue
Asheville, NC 28803
(828) 252-5090

Page 131
utensil:
Sabre
Paris, France

Thanks to the following homeowners:

Susan Huff
Mr. and Mrs. Thomas Merrill, Sr.
Alice Schlesser